THE SMUGGLING WAR

The Smuggling War

The Government's Fight against Smuggling in the 18th and 19th Centuries

Geoffrey Morley

ALAN SUTTON PUBLISHING LIMITED

First published in the United Kingdom in 1994
Alan Sutton Publishing Ltd · Phoenix Mill · Far Thrupp · Stroud
Gloucestershire

First published in the United States of America in 1994
Alan Sutton Publishing Inc. · 83 Washington Street · Dover · NH 03820

British Library Cataloguing in Publication Data
A catalogue record for this book is available from the British Library.

ISBN 0-7509-0349-X

Library of Congress Cataloging in Publication Data applied for

Typeset in 11/14 Bembo.
Typesetting and origination by
Alan Sutton Publishing Limited.
Printed in Great Britain by
Butler & Tanner, Frome, Somerset.

CONTENTS

This book is dedicated to
June, Sophie, Matthew, Susanna and Tony

ILLUSTRATIONS

ACKNOWLEDGEMENTS

I am very grateful to the following for their help: the Public Records Office for the Act of August, 1661, Crown Copyright, reference SP 16/541; Ian Wright and the staff of HM Customs and Excise Library Services, New King's Beam House, London, particularly for permission to use 'General Instructions for the Coast Guard of the United Kingdom: 1829'; Gail Kerr and the staff of HM Customs and Excise HQ, Manchester Records Unit PDD4 for illustrations; Graham Smith; Dr Mary Waugh; Conway Maritime Press for the portrait of William Arnold, and Arnold's letters; Hampshire County Council and the Red House Museum staff in Christchurch, Dorset, for the Marryat letter; and the County Records Office of Dorset, Dorchester.

Reproduction of Ogden's Cigarette Cards by kind permission of Imperial Publishing Limited.

GEOFFREY MORLEY

The map shows the main entrepôts on the Continent, and the principal
smuggling communities in Britain

CHAPTER ONE

THE GOLDEN AGE

The shore of the noble promontory Hengistbury Head, at the southern extremity of the united Avon and Stour Rivers, was a spot frequently chosen as a landing-place for the contraband goods. Of this grand feature of the coast our elevated schoolroom commanded a perfect view; and with the assistance of a tolerable glass enabled us to distinguish every moving object on the declivity of Hengistbury Head. . . . I have myself, more than once, seen a procession of twenty or thirty waggons loaded with kegs of spirits, an armed man sitting at the front and tail of each, and surrounded by a troop of two or three hundred horsemen, every one carrying on his enormous saddle from two to four tubs of spirits, winding deliberately and with the utmost picturesque and imposing effect along the skirts of Hengistbury Head, on their way towards the wild country to the north-west of Christchurch, the point of their separation.

The Revenue troop, who always had intelligence of the 'run', were, it is true, present on the occasion, but with no other views and intentions than those of perfect peace. A flood of homely jokes was poured upon them by the passing ruffians; but these were always accompanied by a present of kegs, greater or less, according to the quantity of the smuggled goods, a voluntary toll received, as it was conferred, in perfect good humour and with mutual satisfaction.[1]

The Reverend Richard Warner wrote this in 1830 as he recalled his boyhood as a pupil in the grammar school at Christchurch, Hampshire, which functioned in the loft over the Lady chapel of the great Priory church. He continued his account of the local smugglers during the time he was at the school, from 1776 to 1780, with a description of the smuggling craft they used:

One of these remarkable vessels I well remember, the property of a celebrated adventurer in contraband articles, nick-named 'Slippery' Rogers from his eel-like faculty of escaping the grasp of his maritime pursuers. The measurement of this noble boat, said to be the longest ever constructed, was almost marvellous, it being a hundred and twenty feet from the tip of her bowsprit to the end of her outrigger. She had a cuddy fore and aft for sleeping-berths, and a large open space amidships for the stowage of two or three thousand ankers of spirits. I must candidly confess that the lads of my school never saw this beautiful vessel starting for her adventurous voyage without giving one cheer for her success. The gallant object was, in truth, not a little adapted to stir the youthful fancy. Her unequalled length and perfect symmetry of form, her thousands of square feet of canvas courting the breeze and swelling to the sun; her forty rowers sweeping the rippled surface of the river with strong, well-measured strokes; their careless mirth, their choral songs and triumphant huzzas, mingled with parting salutes and farewell wishes to their friends on shore, combined to produce an effect that might well have moved the spirit of a much graver personage than an imaginative youth who had seen only his eleventh or twelfth year.

Warner's recollection may have been tinged with the romantic haze which was fast surrounding smuggling in the 1830s, but this must have been a fairly accurate picture of the golden age for the English

One of the early riding officers of Customs

contraband trade. This period, so delightfully redolent of Gilbert and Sullivan, also, however, had its reverse side. The following newspaper report published on 19 March 1779, the year before Warner left school, illustrates this:

> On Friday . . . the Excise Officer at Cranborne in Dorset, having intelligence of upwards of twenty horses, loaded with smuggled goods, passing by that place, he with six dragoons quartered in Cranborne, armed with guns, swords, pistols, etc., went in pursuit of them, and, about four o'clock in the afternoon finding the goods in a coppice near Hook's Wood in the Parish of Farnham, they immediately seized them, loaded their horses and began to carry them away; upon which the smugglers, who were not far distant, collected themselves to the number of forty or fifty and attacked the dragoons in order to rescue their goods, when a desperate affray ensued. The soldiers with their broadswords behaved with great resolution and bravery. The Excise man, it is said, fired his fusee and wounded one of the smugglers in the arm, so that it must be amputated; another smuggler was shot in the left breast, and the ball went through him. The smugglers made use of large clubs, and, being highly exasperated, dealt their blows about very severely. They were at last victorious; they beat the soldiers in an inhuman manner, broke their swords, demolished their firearms, and carried off their horses in triumph; but they have been all since found. An information having been made on oath that two smugglers were in bed at an inn on the Blandford road, they were taken the next morning by a party of dragoons from Wimborne and committed to Dorchester Gaol. We have just heard that a smuggler is dead of his wounds in the above affray.[2]

English smuggling had started in the reign of King Edward I (1239–1307), when English wool was being bought by French weavers who sold their cloth for lower prices than English textiles commanded. When the king was told of this he immediately levied a tax on all wool and woollen products leaving England. The French merchants were hit hard, until they were approached by certain English traders who offered to supply them with woolstuffs at something like the old prices. These were the English wool-smugglers, or 'owlers', as they came to be called, for they

An officer of Light Dragoons

smuggled their contraband out of England by 'owl-light'. So began the long struggle between the forces of the English Crown and the wool-smugglers of Kent and Sussex.

The actual word 'smuggler' seems to have come into the language during the English civil wars, which lasted from April 1642 until August 1649. After the restoration of King Charles II, a royal proclamation was issued on 9 August 1661, '. . . for the prevention and punishment of all frauds on the Customs committed by . . . a sort of lewd people called "Smuckellors", never heard of before the late disordered times, who make it their trade . . . to steal and defraud His Majesty of His Customs.' There is very little information as to what was being smuggled at this time, apart from the wool still being taken out by the owlers of Kent and Sussex. In 1698, however, another Act of Parliament was put on the statute-book and this created the Landguard of riding officers of the

Customs, who were to combat the owlers; the act also put strict controls on the trading in wool and wool products within 15 miles of the coast.

The beginning of the eighteenth century saw a great increase in smuggling as tea, tobacco, spirits and luxuries had duties levied on them, thereby making them worth smuggling. As it perceived the rising level of smuggling and consequent defrauding of 'His Majesty of His Customs', the government of the day brought in Acts of Parliament to stop the

The Prize: the hull of a seized smuggling vessel, if not needed by the Royal Navy or Customs, was sawn into pieces and many ended up like this, still doing a useful job

illegal practice. In 1717 smugglers who refused to plead guilty were to be transported overseas; and in the next year the first of what became known as 'the hovering Acts' was passed. This was designed to discourage small, shallow-draught boats from approaching the shore. A vessel under 15 tons found to be carrying tea, brandy, pepper or French silk, for example, found hovering within 6 miles of the British coast was liable to be seized by the king's ships, providing she was not waiting for wind and weather to improve in her favour. When this Act did not work, another was brought in three years later, in which the upper burden was raised to 40 tons, and boats with four or more oars found near the coast, or on the River Thames below London Bridge, were to be seized and sawn into three pieces of equal size. Ship-sized vessels taken were to be burned. Anyone buying or receiving smuggled goods could be fined or imprisoned for three months. The penalty for smuggling itself was now to be transportation for seven years '. . . to His Majesty's Plantations and Colonies in America'; but many returned to the work when they came home, for they knew they were marked men and had little to lose. The term 'smuggling' was redefined, so that there could be no mistake when cases came to court, as follows: running goods without paying duty; doing so with more than five persons in a company; carrying offensive weapons while doing so; wearing any vizard, mask or other disguise while running contraband; or forcibly resisting officers of the Customs and Excise when they were trying to seize smuggled goods.

Such severe measures, however, only made the smugglers more desperate than they were before, the usual consequence of almost all the anti-smuggling legislation of the period. As a result, after a host of pleas from all parts of the coastal counties, in 1723 the government decided to post units of dragoons at strategic points along the shores. These soldiers were ideal for pitting against the worst smugglers, for they were not true cavalry but heavy infantry on horseback who rode fast into battle, usually dismounted and then fought on foot, as seen in the earlier account of the Battle of Hook's Wood in Dorset. Their main weapon was the carbine, a short-barrelled musket designed specifically for use on horseback, which gave them a great advantage over the smugglers with their usual haphazard assortment of firearms. The government gave the riding officers of Customs authority to require, rather than request, the co-operation of these dragoons whenever they suspected a smuggling run was about to be made.

One of the greatest parliamentarians to pit himself personally against the smugglers was Sir Robert Walpole. He firmly believed that the only answer to the growing national menace of smuggling was to scrap all the existing laws and start afresh. Tobacco and spirits were the commodities most frequently run by the smugglers, so in 1733 he proposed an Excise, rather than a Customs scheme under which tobacco and spirits would be imported quite freely, but put straight from ship into bonded warehouse until distributed; at which point the Excise tax would be slapped on. Walpole had realized that Excise officers were far more efficient than Customs men; but the word 'excise' was, in the minds of Englishmen, connected with two hated regimes: the commonwealth of England under the Cromwells, and the government of France. There arose a howl of execration from all classes when Walpole outlined his proposals and protests got so bad that the government thought civil war was going to break out. The wise Walpole bowed gracefully to the inevitable saying: 'In the present inflamed temper of the people the Act could not be carried into execution without an armed force!' When his decision became public bonfires were lit in the streets, people danced round them for joy, and the bells were rung in churches the length and breadth of the land.[3]

However, Walpole was not going to let the smugglers get away with it: he immediately appointed a committee to look deeply into the situation and put at its head as chairman the famous general Sir John Cope, later to be thrashed by the Scots at the Battle of Prestonpans, but at this time better known as an implacable foe of English smugglers. The committee's White Paper said:

The smugglers being grown to such a degree of insolence as to carry on their wicked practices by force and violence, not only in the country and remote parts of the Kingdom, but even in the City of London itself, going in gangs armed with swords, pistols and other weapons, even to the number of forty or fifty, by which means they have been too strong, not only for the Officers of the Revenue but for the civil magistrates themselves. . . . The number of Custom House Officers who have been beaten, abused and wounded since Christmas

1723 being no less than 250, besides six others who have been actually murdered in the execution of their duty.[4]

So in 1736 there appeared 'An Act for the Indemnifying of persons who have been found guilty of offences against the laws made for securing the revenues of Customs and Excise, and for enforcing those laws for the future.' The main provisions of this severe Act were the death penalty for so much as wounding a king's officer, for using arms against one, for resisting arrest when unarmed and even for so much as hindering an officer in the execution of his duty. There were also lesser penalties for these offences: five years' transportation, flogging, a month's hard labour or impressment into the Royal Navy. Once convicted, a free pardon could be offered if the smuggler confessed all past offences and informed on his colleagues. If a reformed smuggler, however, returned to his old ways and was caught, all the offences he had ever committed would be brought up against him, even those for which he had already been pardoned. These would then be counted as second offences, while those with whom he was caught would be regarded as first offenders, with transportation as their punishment; but for second offenders it was death by the rope. For bribing either Customs or Excise officers there was a £50 fine; ale-house keepers who harboured smugglers were to be fined and ordered to surrender their victuallers' licences. On land anyone found 'lurking' within 5 miles of the coast or a navigable river and obviously not on lawful business would be taken before the nearest magistrate and given a month's hard labour if found guilty. At sea transferring cargo from one ship to another within 12 miles of the shore was an offence; and anyone on shore making warning signals, either by day or night, to a known smuggling vessel was also liable to arrest. If a vessel was found within 5 miles of the coast with more than the specified amount of brandy or tea, its master had to be able to prove that duty had been paid on the commodities. Any unable to do so were liable to transportation to the Colonies in America.

It was a tough act, with severe penalties, and its precision in terms of distances from the coast must have sharpened up the smugglers' navigational skills considerably. Certainly, it had little other effect on the contraband trade: it was to be one more of Sir John Cope's defeats. So by 1745 yet another parliamentary enquiry was deemed necessary, and this found that in Sussex, one of the worst smuggling counties next to its neighbour Kent, 1,835 horse-loads of tea and 1,689 horse-loads of brandy had recently been landed in the space of six months. 20,000 men were smuggling along the Sussex coast, it was discovered. As for Kent, the Hawkhurst Gang, the most notorious smuggling outfit ever, could assemble 500 men in an hour, the enquiry was told, among other horrifying revelations of the strength of the smugglers. When it came the new Act was more Draconian than ever: smuggling was now declared a felony punishable alone by hanging. It was also a felony to assemble for the purpose of running contraband and even to harbour smugglers, the penalty again being death. When serious offences provoked by smuggling happened, collective fines were to be imposed on the districts in which they took place, and the reward for informing on the 'free traders', as they called themselves, was raised to £500. There was also 'Gazetting': the names of known smugglers were published in *The London Gazette* (though how many of them read this journal is open to question) and those so honoured could either surrender in forty days or be attainted for felony. The same applied to the Customs Board's many posters. Such half-baked ideas simply ensured that the smugglers fought even more ferociously when they were cornered as capture meant automatic death at the hands of the hangman. The gangs' strangleholds on their districts grew ever tighter, and when an informer did relay information the smugglers' revenge was worse than before: death rather than abduction.

Only one measure had any real effect: the lowering of tea-duty in that same year, 1745. Illegal profits dropped sharply and the contrabandists were exceedingly angry. In fact, the Hawkhurst Gang was so incensed that when a cargo of tea they had been waiting for was seized at sea and lodged in the Poole Customs House, they came across four counties and stole it out of sheer pique. Sales of legal tea naturally rose sharply for the whole nation was now addicted to the pernicious weed. This must have pleased that notorious tea-drinker Dr Samuel Johnson, the foremost literary figure of the age, whose kettle was 'never off the boil'. He was freed of any conscientious pangs of double standards when he wrote in his great *Dictionary* that a smuggler was: 'A wretch who, in defiance of the law, imports and exports goods without payment of Customs.'

Other theorists were turning their minds to the problem of smuggling around this time. Cesare Beccaria, the coiner of the famous phrase 'the greatest happiness of the greatest number' (though not for smugglers), wrote in his *Treatise on Crimes and Punishments* of 1768: 'Smuggling, though a real offence, is owing to the laws themselves, for the higher the duties the greater the advantage and consequently the temptation.' And Adam Smith, himself no less than a commissioner of Customs, put it in this way: 'A smuggler is a person who, although no doubt blameable for violating the laws of the country, is frequently incapable of violating those of natural justice, and would have been in every respect an excellent citizen had not his country made that a crime which nature never meant to be so.'[5] Dangerous words were these, which showed that the smugglers' apologists were not confined to their own class. It was the puckish Charles Lamb who, many years later, was to write: 'I like a smuggler! He is the only honest thief. He robs nothing but the Revenue, an abstraction I never greatly cared about!'[6]

So much for the theorists; but that eminently practical man John Wesley, the founder of Methodism, and preaching throughout the country at this time, had no doubts about smuggling's iniquity. Wherever he met the practice he raised his courageous voice. The people of Rye, he said, '. . . will not part with the accursed thing: smuggling! So, I fear, with these our labour will be in vain. . . . One sin allowed would intercept the whole blessing.' His words had gone before him when, in 1751, he reached St Ives in Cornwall. The local smugglers were ready for him and hurled abuse, rotten eggs and even stones at the fearless Christian, but he kept on preaching against smuggling and believed he had had some effect. Certainly when he returned eleven years later he wrote: 'What a change is wrought! That detestable practice of cheating the King is no more found in our societies. And since that accursed thing is put away the work of God has everywhere increased.'[7] Wesley would not even touch tea and advised all his followers to give up 'that slow poison', as he called it. It is said by some that it was only the spread of Methodism that prevented England from falling completely under the smugglers' rule.

Wesley, however, had been misled: smuggling continued unabated, and in 1748 the Army agreed, under pressure from the Board of Customs, to assign some of its finest regiments to the seaboard counties. Standing orders were carefully laid down to combat the 'accursed thing' effectively. Eight regiments of the best cavalry, five heavy and three light, were sent to the south and east coasts; and in each regiment a subaltern was given a small troop which he had to place at the disposal of the chief riding officer in the area. This ensign was also required to acquaint himself thoroughly with his sector, and study the roads, bridle-paths and footpaths so that his work with the Revenue men would be of the highest efficiency. The new standing orders also stipulated that no fewer than twelve soldiers under the designated subaltern or his NCO had to be placed at the Revenue officer's disposal immediately he asked for assistance. The Army even provided an extra allowance for fodder on this duty; and prize-money from seizures made was, by order, to be shared by every man in the regiment.

A system of fining counties for smuggling activities had also just been introduced: £200 if a seizure was made by the king's men and no smugglers were captured; and the fine to be remitted if the smugglers involved were captured in the ensuing six months. The fine for a king's officer being killed in the county was a mere £100, and just £40 for knocking one unconscious. However, capturing a smuggler was worth an award of £500 to the county.

In 1746 the death penalty was brought in as the punishment for the mere act of assembling for the purpose of running contraband. Such a terrible change from the deterrent of transportation was due to the fact that Britain was at war in this year, which always made the government stiffer in its resolve. In addition, harbouring smugglers was now to be a capital offence; and to force juries in the smuggling counties to convict their free-trading brethren, fines were to be levied if known offenders were not convicted within six months. Another county fine was imposed for seized goods that had been recovered by force by the smugglers, the amount being £200. A system of rewards and pardons was brought in for 'stool-pigeons' willing to betray two or more accomplices, a measure given a trial period of seven years, but one which remained in force until 1826.

William Pitt the Younger hated smuggling but he was in a better position to do something about it than others of his time: he became prime minister. Among the papers of Lord Shelburne, home secretary in 1782, is a report[8] made in 1784 by Pitt, in which sweeping changes to the anti-smuggling laws were strongly proposed. Pitt wrote:

The manner in which smuggled goods are protected in the landing, and afterwards disposed of is yet a more serious and alarming consideration, for it appears by the reports of our Collectors that in all the maritime counties the strength and number of the men employed in that business is indeed very formidable, insomuch that in some districts they are capable of assembling from five hundred to a thousand men on any extraordinary occasion; and that on ordinary occasions the numbers collected to receive the goods on the sea coast is greater or less according to the quantity, and the greater or less probability of resistance; but in general greatly beyond anything that can be brought to oppose them . . .

As always, Pitt was concerned with the effect of smuggling on the economic well-being of his country, for he went on:

The case is exactly similar with regard to the public dealers in spiritous liquors, and the effect will be seen in comparison of the duties upon spirits, coffee and tea in 1766 with the duties upon the same articles in 1776. In the former period they amounted to £1,114,677 12s. 0¼d.; in the latter to no more than £1,060,391 5s. 6d., a *decrease*, which, considering the *increase* of population and the growing consumption of tea by all ranks of people, is an evidence of the great increase of smuggling. . . .

Pitt did not work alone, however: he, Lord Shelburne, Adam Smith and even Edmund Burke turned their formidable talents to the problem of curbing the free traders. For the truth was it had become a national disgrace and was beginning to make Britain a laughing-stock throughout the world. They looked at such abuses as the rampant buying and selling of commissions in the Customs service; the flagrant nepotism; the many sinecures; the low salaries and the bribery and corruption they encouraged; and the way in which the highest posts went to county families, bankrupt merchants and retired Army and Royal Navy officers, who had no interest in the Customs service and were too old to learn the ropes. The four examiners were appalled at the complex nature of the Customs system of accounting, wide open to all kinds of fiddling and fraud. In addition they found that smuggling had recently increased

A political cartoon of 1787 on the occasion of William Pitt's simplification
and consolidation of the Customs and Excise duties. The middle figure,
apparently Pitt, says:
'Come, boys, since they say we have well begun,
Let's bear hard 'till the whole's comprest in one.'
(HM Customs & Excise)

threefold in many notorious places; and that contraband smuggled in north of the River Humber and west of the River Tamar was mainly sold locally, most of the rest going to London. As a result, Burke recommended the reduction of the duty on tea, and Smith, who was at this time a Scottish commissioner of Customs, pointed out that a tax of 1d., which it would not be worth anyone's while to avoid, was better than a tax of 1s., which would not produce any revenue as everyone would smuggle like mad to avoid paying it. Pitt was enormously impressed by these ideas, and so when he was appointed to be the king's chief minister in 1784 he was more than ready to take on the smugglers with the force of some new laws.

His resolve was stiffened further, if it needed to be, by his own calculations, made as he took stock in his new office. Over 13 million lb of tea, he saw, were consumed in England each year but only 5½ million had duty paid on them: it was as simple as that. He also discovered that the Exchequer lost £3 million each year in unpaid tobacco duty. 10,000 guineas were spent by the English smugglers each week when they went shopping for their contraband, he was told by his officials.[9] Pitt acted straight away, and the 'Hovering Act' which he brought in that same year, 1784, was a good deal more sensible than many of its predecessors. Any vessel hovering within 3 miles of the English coast and having cargoes of spirits in casks of less than 60 gallons was forfeit to the Crown. All vessels, whether lugger, cutter or galley, having obviously been built specifically for smuggling were to be carefully examined and their owners made to promise that they would not be used for this purpose. This was done on oath and a licence issued as evidence. An owner not making this oath had his vessel immediately seized, of course. Penalties were made more severe: shooting at anti-smuggling patrols, whether Revenue or Royal Navy personnel were wounded or killed or not, was a capital offence, and the trick often employed by smuggling captains of flying Admiralty colours or Customs House pennants to mislead pursuers was to be punished by a fine of £500. A Customs officer accepting a bribe was to be fined the same amount.

Effective as many of these sensible measures were, Pitt's best idea was cutting duty: on French wines it went down from £90 3s. 10d. a tun to £43 1s. per tun; and he slashed the tea-duty, Burke's favourite target, from 119 per cent to an amazing 12 per cent. This tea tax now had to be paid on the price it fetched in the sales held by the East India Company, which had to account to the government. This measure had an almost immediate effect and tea ceased to be worth smuggling.

Parliament had hoped that Pitt would have the same impact on the traffic in tobacco as he had done for tea, for the smugglers were diddling the Exchequer out of £3 million each year on their contraband. It was not until 1789, however, that Pitt brought in a scheme which allowed the weed to be imported in ships over 120 tons that carried packages of not less than 450 lb. He confined the tobacco trade to London, Bristol, Glasgow, Liverpool and seven other designated ports, in which it was to go straight from the ships into bonded warehouses. Here it passed into the care of the officers of the Excise who would issue the essential permits for sale.

William Pitt's hatred of the smugglers was well shown in January 1785, less than a year after he took up office. Knowing his constant interest in their doings, someone told him that the recent heavy gales had forced the smugglers in the Channel ports to pull their boats up onto the beaches out of harm's way. Pitt saw his chance to strike simply and ruthlessly: he singled out Deal as his target, the worst smuggling town in the whole kingdom. He asked for a regiment to be sent there on the pretext of holding an exercise, but the commanding officer had special orders. The regiment was billeted in a barn overnight as all the inn signs had been taken down and no Deal house would accept the soldiers. The next morning the foot regiment was on the beach, and a number of Revenue vessels were noticed by the locals just off the shore. Idly they looked on, waiting for the manoeuvres to begin, rather amused, if anything. But when a bugle call rang out the infantrymen charged across the shingle for the boats drawn up on their blocks, and when they reached them they set to work with their tinder-boxes. The smugglers and townspeople of Deal suddenly realized what was happening but they were powerless to act as fire engulfed every one of the vessels on the beach. There were so many soldiers that 'the inhabitants were obliged to remain silent spectators, and dared not attempt a rescue', as one eye-witness wrote later. All they could do was to make an effigy of the prime minister and hurl it onto the bonfire made of their boats. Deal never forgot nor forgave the statesman who

This cartoon was published in 1819 and depicts John Bull again, this time
visited by the new taxes about which he exclaims: 'Who the devil would
have thought of seeing you after I've paid you so often? Well, I see there is
no trusting anybody!' (HM Customs & Excise)

had got his own back on the smugglers of 'this infernal town', as Pitt had
put it.

William Pitt had 'laboured harder than any man to prevent the fair
trader being hurt by the smugglers', and he had evolved great plans for
the reform of tariffs which would have established truly free trade. But in
1793 war with the French broke out and those plans had to be shelved.
Smuggling on a greater scale than ever before was immediately triggered,
and free trade had to wait until the 1820s, for Pitt died in 1806 and the
wars went on until Napoleon was finally beaten at Waterloo in 1815.

CHAPTER TWO

THE 'THIN BLUE LINE'

The success of anti-smuggling legislation, was, of course, always dependent upon the men who had to enforce its provisions. For no matter how brilliant the plans of the generals, in war it is the quality of the ordinary soldiers and sailors in the front line which determines the outcome of the conflict.

The 'infantry' in this war could be said to have been the riding officers of the Customs service: the Landguard was established as early as 1699 to combat the exporting of wool from England. The salary was quite good, and was supplemented by expenses for a servant. Each riding officer had a 10 mile beat of coast to patrol, and they were posted from the Isle of Sheppey round the coast to the Port of Chichester. Over them, as their surveyor-general, was the man who had thought up the idea, Captain Henry Baker. He was the first in a long line of zealous Customs officers, most of whom made a real contribution to stemming the ever-rising flow of contraband. The effect of their work lasted a short while but only drastic legislation to lower duties could bring the smuggling war to an end in the long run.

Captain Henry Baker thought he had done the trick in the year 1703 when he wrote to his masters sitting on the Board of Customs: 'I do believe the neck of this owling trade is in great measure broke, especially in Romney Marsh, as well as the spirit of the owlers.'[1] He was, to a large extent, right: wool was declining as the sole and staple commodity of the export smugglers, but this only gave way to the trickle of incoming contraband which was so soon to grow to an undamnable flood.

London was, even at this early date, giving the Customs Board cause for concern, and special officers had to be appointed: known as land carriage men, their job was to examine carriages drawing up at the inns of the metropolis to see that no smuggled goods were being carried. Soon more were appointed at the other big ports of the country, with

powers to search inns and their outbuildings for goods which they
suspected had been smuggled out of the ports along the land routes
which the carriages covered. Excise officers were given similar powers
soon after: now both Customs and Excise men could board ships in the
ports to rummage through them for the growing amounts of liquor
being added to the smugglers' ever-growing shopping lists. Both sides
were squaring up for the warfare soon to break out nationwide.

In 1718 the shape of things to come manifested itself at King's Lynn in
Norfolk. Customs officers surprised smugglers landing a cargo of brandy,
chased them off and lodged the contraband in the Customs House. The
smugglers returned, determined to recover their goods and whipped up
the townsfolk, always sympathetic, even then, to riot. So bad did the
situation become that the magistrates had to call out the local militia to
restore order and arrest as many rioters and smugglers as they could.

It was in 1698 that the Customs Board put into commission a fleet of
sloops to sail a Waterguard round the coasts of the whole country to
assist the work of the Landguard of riding officers. These were purely
Customs vessels, the forerunners of the famous cutters of later fame, and
were not under Admiralty control. It was in the direction and skilful use
of such ships that another outstanding Customs officer made his
reputation in manning the 'thin blue line' facing the smugglers. His
name was Warren Lisle, a Dorset man born in 1699, the son of a
Revenue officer. He was appointed patent searcher in the port of Poole
at the age of seventeen; and his first noted success was the seizure of a
small smuggling vessel at Portland. We know little of his career up until
he is called 'Captain' Lisle in a Customs Board letter: clearly he had
made a name for himself in this time. He then went ashore and became
supervisor of riding officers in the Weymouth Customs district; in 1734
he commanded the Revenue sloop *Walker*, which he had bought from
the Crown and refurbished from his own pocket. In 1737 Lisle seized
the *Guernsey Packet*, a cutter which had been smuggling under cover of
her legitimate duty! This he refitted and renamed *Beehive*. He was
getting much busier as the years passed. Lisle got another ship and with
this little squadron soon had the seas from Hengistbury Head to Start
Point well covered. In 1738 *Beehive* caught a smuggling sloop off
Portland, and pursued it for over five hours before being able to overtake
her. With the assistance of a nearby Royal Navy cutter, the *Diamond*, he

managed to put a party aboard. However, the smugglers managed to overpower its members and nail them up in the cabin, turning out toward the sea and freedom. The smugglers landed the king's men in France, as was usual, and Lisle had to go across and negotiate their release, as well as that of the *Diamond*'s captain.

In 1739 Captain Lisle was chosen as surveyor of the sloops for the South Coast by the Board of Customs, and his command now stretched from Portsmouth to Land's End. Lisle was frequently called upon by his masters for his advice on everything in the service from staffing to the design of better vessels with which to chase the smugglers, for the war against them was really hotting up. As his flagship he was given a brand new sloop called the *Cholmondley*, at 80 tons the largest Revenue vessel afloat.

In 1745 Lisle moved his headquarters to Lyme Regis in Dorset, even then a fashionable resort, where he was able to house himself as a gentleman from the proceeds of the many seizures he and his sloops were making. In 1748 he was honoured by being made a 'capital' burgess of the town, and in 1751 he became mayor, a title he bore twice more in his life. Lisle bought several more ships for his fleet, and the Board sent him to examine charges of maladministration in such places as Plymouth and Penzance, where he found that collectors had been working with the smugglers for years.

In 1779 Warren Lisle retired from the Customs service which he had served so long and faithfully, mainly in order to express his thoughts on how that service could be improved. He wrote a series of reports for Lord Shelburne, the home secretary, supplementing the work of that other great foe of smuggling, William Pitt, and detailing not only the state of the illicit trade but also the extent of the corruption which so crippled the service, robbing it of its full fighting efficiency. Lisle died in 1788. Below is Lisle's letter to the home secretary, written in August 1782:

The Smuggling Trade, between the Isle of Wight and St Alban's Point, is now carried on in large armed cutters and luggers, all manned with English, Dutch, French and American sailors, from Dunkirk or Ostend, with a French commission and large cargoes of tea, Geneva and Brandy, few less than £3,000 value the first cost. Two Revenue cutters to guard this station; that from Southampton makes some good seizures, the other from Poole very few, and I am well informed owing to the master, mate and crews being corrupted; and certain signals now in my possession, the latter withdraws to another part of the coast to give opportunities to the smugglers to land and carry off their cargoes without interruption, though sometimes they are bribed with a few casks to save appearances. Very often no less than twenty waggons to carry off their cargoes, frequently whole cargoes of Portugal, Spanish and French wines.

The traders from St Alban's Point to the Berry Head ply in smaller cutters and have their cargoes from Alderney; our Revenue cutters for the guard of this station who agree with the smugglers, and content themselves with a small share from the smugglers, suffer the greater part to be run ashore.

Those who carry on the business from the Berry Head to the Ram Head generally buy their cargoes at Guernsey, sometimes at Roscoff at the mouth of the Morlaix River in France and bring over large cargoes of tea and brandy in fine-sailing lugsail vessels, that the Waterguard makes few seizures. When they have landed their cargoes the shore officers are too much their friends to give them trouble.

Between the Ram Head and Manacles the business is carried on to a very great degree from Guernsey and Roscoff, and much done in Falmouth Harbour, especially up the river that leads to Truro, the Officers of all ranks too nearly related and too much connected to give offence to the neighbouring boroughs . . .

From the Manacles to the Land's End, and chiefly in Mount's Bay, is a most notorious trade of smuggling of large cargoes from Roscoff and Guernsey, whole cargoes of wine landed in the very harbours of Penzance, Markell Jew, Newlyn, Porthleven, Coverack, etc., which must be done with the connivance of the superior, as well as the inferior, officers, who are all promoted by members of the little Cornish boroughs and protected from being turned out.

. . . As the smuggling trade can never be wholly suppressed, I take leave to observe . . . that if the commanders of the Revenue cutters were prevented from compounding with the smugglers for a certain share of the cargo given them; for suffering large ones to be landed, obliged to give a faithful account, and seize every vessel and boat forfeited by the Hovering Act, and the names of those who are aiding and assisting, prosecute them for the penalties, and no composition accepted by the Commissioners of the Customs and Excise, which has been frequently done for trifles; the seamen on board the smuggling vessels impressed and immediately put on board our ships-of-war; and in default of the officers doing their duty to make examples by turning out a few, it would greatly distress the smuggling business. The tidesmen and enforcer officers who are put on board merchant-ships are in general corrupted, and often assist in running and bringing ashore large quantities, without payment of duties, for which they receive large gratuities and live like gentlemen in their house, which cannot be done for £30 or £40 per annum.

I humbly recommend the giving of deputations without any salaries to some of the commanders of the sloops-of-war who are stationed on the coast, who are able to engage those daring smugglers that infest it. A very fine sailing one is just appointed for the protection of the trade on this coast, the most promising vessel for sailing I ever saw, called the *Orestes*, Captain John Hope Bowers. She was one of those taken by Captain Mackbride of the *Artois*, and I dare say would soon give a good account of those on his cruising-station. I have this day sent 35 fine sailors to Deptford to assist in bringing her round and shall use my best endeavour to procure as many volunteers as in my power to man the *Orestes*. . . .[2]

Lisle's unpolished style reveals a man not afraid to speak his mind, even suggesting malpractice by the commissioners of the Customs and Excise, and making practical suggestions right up to the end, even after he has left the service in which he so excelled.

Lisle knew very well, none better, that it was no picnic captaining the king's cutters: Captain Brisac, commander of the *Speedwell* stationed at Poole in Dorset, a veritable hotbed of smuggling, received two letters in the year 1790. The first was in verse and ran:

> Thou damn'd Bursack!
> I'll break thy back
> When I see thee again!
> And if I don't
> Depend upon't
> I'll kill one of thy men!
>   Dick.

The other was in rough prose:

> Damn thee and God damn thy two publind eyes, thou Bugger and
> thou death-looking son-of-a-bitch! Oh, that I had been there with my
> company for thy sake when thou tookest men of mine on board the
> *Speedwell* cutter on Monday, 14th December! I would cross thee and thy
> gang to hell where thou belong'st, thou devil incarnate. Go down, thou
> hellhound, into thy kennel below, and bathe thyself in that sulphurous
> lake that has for so long prepared for such as thee; for it is time the
> world was rid of such a monster! Thou art no man but a devil, thou
> fiend! O Lucifer, I hope that thou will soon fall into hell like a star from
> the sky, there to be unpitied and unrelented of any for ever and ever!
>   Which God grant of His infinite Mercy. Amen.
>   J. Spurier,
>   Fordingbridge,
>   January . . . fast asleep.[3]

William Arnold was another South Coast officer whose contribution to
the struggle with the ever-growing smuggling problem stood out far
above those of his contemporaries. If only there had been more
commanders of the stature of Lisle and Arnold further east along the
coast, then smuggling might have been brought under control before the
terrible wars against Napoleon.

Arnold, whose son was to make his name as the great headmaster of
Rugby School, was appointed collector of Customs for the Isle of Wight
on 30 September 1777, just a year after the outbreak of the war with
America. His former experience in the Post Office gave him a meticulous
attention to detail; and he found that the position of collector made him
the virtual king of the island. The Wight was a smugglers' paradise, many
of its villagers doing no work other than running contraband, so that they
slept all day and smuggled all night. On 3 March 1779, having examined
the situation very thoroughly, Arnold wrote to his masters, the
commissioners of the Board of Customs at Billingsgate in London:

> Honourable Sirs,
>   There is now building at Cowes a boat between sixty and seventy
> feet long, and about eighteen feet wide, intended to row with twenty

William Arnold, Collector of Customs in the Isle of Wight from 1777 until his death in 1801

oars and to carry sail occasionally. She is evidently intended for the purpose of smuggling only, and belongs, as we are informed, to a reputed smuggler. Several of these boats have been seen lately on these coasts, and they have so much the advantage of fast rowing and sailing that we apprehend that but few of the Revenue cutters can come up with them.

We therefore humbly beg leave to submit to your Honours'
consideration whether it may not be proper to apply to the
legislature that the Act by which all boats or barges for rowing, built
to row with more than four oars, found within the counties of
Middlesex, Surrey, Kent and Essex are forfeited, may not be
extended to other counties.

Like Lisle, Arnold, although by no means a sailor, realized the vital
importance of using ships and boats in the war against the smugglers.
When his masters offered him more men he replied that he would rather
have more boats for the Waterguard to work with the Landguard of
riding officers, showing his clear appreciation of how to use his forces.
Specifically, he asked for a cutter, a second request, continuing in a letter
of October 1783:

> Stationing a frigate with a King's cutter in Studland Bay, and a King's
> cutter also in Hurst Road(s), may probably be of service for the
> Revenue cruisers occasionally to resort to for assistance. And if they
> serve to keep off the large cutters from landing their goods for three
> or four days at a time, it would go far, we apprehend, to ruin the
> Trade, because the expense of keeping a large number of men and
> horses together waiting the arrival of goods must materially diminish
> the profits arising from their sale.

Again in the same month he wrote: 'We beg leave to report that within
the last three years smuggling has increased upon this coast to an
alarming degree. Illicit trade is principally carried on in large armed
cutters or luggers from two to three hundred tons burthen, with which
the Revenue cruisers are not able to contend. . . .'

Clearly, the war was going the smugglers' way at this time. Arnold
continued:

> It is no unusual thing for them to land their goods in open day under
> protection of their guns, sometimes in sight of Revenue cutters whom
> they will not suffer to come near or board them. [It will be recalled
> that Richard Warner's eye-witness account of the Christchurch
> smugglers just after they had landed their contraband 'in open day'

The Revenue cutter *Badger* (HM Customs & Excise)

happened just three years earlier.] The war [against American colonies] gave a sanction to the arming of these vessels, as the masters took out commissions as privateers, tho' in fact they followed no other trade than smuggling. Now the war is over they continue their illicit practices. [Did the Admiralty imagine that these 'privateers' intended to cross the Atlantic to attack the erring colonials?] These large vessels convoy over other smaller ones. They keep off till towards night, when they run in and land their cargoes at places where gangs of smugglers sometimes to the number of 200–300 meet them.

Goods are often landed out of large deep boats carrying 500 to 1,000 casks which have been unshipped at sea from the importing

'The *Greyhound* Excise cutter, Capt. Wm. Watson, on a wind, chasing',
with her guns in action, and working with another king's cutter in the
background (HM Customs & Excise)

vessels. As soon as seen by a Revenue cruiser, they drop the boat
astern, which immediately rows off whilst the commander of the
Revenue cutter is pursuing the vessel he supposes to be loaded. When
he comes up to his great disappointment he finds no cargo on board.

To such a regular science is smuggling now reduced that we are
informed that the smugglers have started prices for their goods in
proportion to the distances they bring them. If they sell at sea to small
coasting vessels or boats, the price of a four gallon cask is about half a
guinea; if landed on shore between Hurst and Christchurch under the
protection of their guns and put into quiet possession of the land

smugglers, fourteen shillings or fifteen shillings a cask; if brought within the Isle of Wight, to Langstone or Portsmouth, the price advances to a guinea a cask.

However, despite all Arnold's letters to London, by April 1791 he was writing: 'Smugglers in general are become more daring than ever, and more frequently assemble in numbers, carrying arms and in disguise. Instances occur very often of officers being wounded, beaten, opposed and obstructed in the execution of their duty, particularly in their attempts to make seizures of run goods.'

Arnold was so keen to combat the smugglers that when Revenue cutters were not forthcoming he paid for the contracting of a series of cutters so that the smugglers would not have it all their own way. Also, his deep interest in their methods led Arnold to realize that the smugglers had, by 1789, taken to using methods of deception which are generally supposed to have come in only in the period of the Napoleonic wars and after. He wrote in that year:

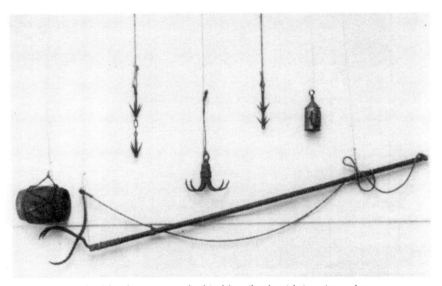

Smugglers' hardware: a standard 'tub' or 'keg', with its wire and rope
carrying tackle; a 15 ft long grab for recovering barrels temporarily hidden
in shallow water such as ponds; a dark lantern and a grapnel and two
'creepers' used for fishing up sunken rafts of kegs from the sea

It is not so much the practice, we believe, on this coast to sink goods as it is to the westward of Portland, where the smugglers usually sink their cargoes on their first coming over from Guernsey or Alderney, and leave them afterwards to be taken up by fishing boats and others who know by certain marks where to find them.

With regard to cordage used by vessels in the smuggling trade for sinking warps, such as is proper for a vessel's hawser or tow line is fit for use. And a boat's grapnel is often used for creeping up goods previously sunk.

It is the practice for many vessels passing for fishing and pilot vessels, to carry with them a large number of sinking stones which they pretend are ballast, and when slung they allege it is for greater convenience in shifting them to windward as occasion may require.

The slings with which small casks of spirits are slung is twice laid cordage, made up with six, or sometimes nine yarns, and exported in large quantities from this country. When fastened round a cask, sufficient length is left over to fasten a sinking stone to, or when landed upon the shore to assist the more easy removal of the casks, whether across the shoulders or on horseback.

Arnold's eye for detail and his precision in description are well shown here.

By the late 1780s Arnold had put together a fine squadron of anti-smuggling ships, mainly by tirelessly nagging his masters, and even the huge smuggling luggers and cutters which had so alarmed him when he first took up his post dared not show themselves in the waters round the Isle of Wight. On land he made sure the patrols were efficient and continually inspected them in person, like any good general does with his front-line troops. Having made sure every inch of his coast was covered, Arnold turned his attention to the fort commanding Sandown Bay and made certain the guns there would be used to assist his efforts against the enemy should he ever call upon them. The Wight must have been one of the most difficult Customs districts to direct, for the islanders were not only an independent race, as they are even today, but were also heavily committed to smuggling. In 1793, when Britain was once again at war with France, Arnold's duties were vastly increased, mainly because the island was always 'a frontier place' and a likely focus not only for naval activity but also for forces of foreign invasion. Working with the Army and Royal Navy, William Arnold saw to it that the Wight was ready for anything, that it was a sure base for those forces at sea, and that smuggling was contained. He had the satisfaction in October 1793 of being able to report to London, at the commissioners' request for information, that the illicit trade had decreased in his collection, due, he said, to 'the vigilance and exertions of the commanders of our Revenue cruisers'. However, it was hard work and, quite suddenly, William Arnold died on 3 March 1801, at the early age of fifty-five.[4]

Frederick Marryat is best known as the author of such classics as *The Children of the New Forest, Masterman Ready, Mr Midshipman Easy* and *The Three Midshipmen*, the last of which describes the work of a Royal Naval cutter engaged in the war against the smugglers of Hampshire and Dorset. He drew on his personal experiences in the winter of 1821 when his own sloop, HMS *Rosario*, assisted the Revenue ships. It was in the following year, 1822, that, in the tradition of Warren Lisle, Marryat wrote a letter which he hoped would be of help in the long, continuing war against the smugglers. Being a Royal Naval captain he naturally sent it to his superior, the First Sea Lord.

My Lord,

Having been informed that Government has lately instituted an enquiry into the measures resorted to for the prevention of smuggling, I trust I shall not be deemed presuming if I venture to submit to your Lordship the circumstances that came under my observation during the few months I was employed on that service. In so doing I shall confine myself to the western side of the Channel, a line of coast of which Portland may be considered as the centre extending from Portsmouth to the Start Point. I have taken these two extremes there being comparatively speaking but little smuggling on the English Channel to the westward of the Start, and that which is carried on to the eastward of Portsmouth is from other parts of France and in a different system. I believe I may confidently state that every cargo run on the line of coast above laid down is shipped from the Port of Cherbourg.

It will be necessary first to direct Your Lordship's attention to the system upon which the smuggling is carried on; and secondly to the means at present resorted to for the prevention of it; to consider whether these means are effectual, and, if not, by what measures they may be made more so than they are at present.

Although it will occasionally happen that the several interests are combined, it may be generally considered that there are three parties in this traffic having interests distinct from each other. The first is the owners of the vessel, who receive a freight for her employment which, if she be successful, will, in a short period, repay the whole expense of building and fitting out. The second is the crew of smugglers hired to sail in the vessel who are paid so many shillings per tub, provided that the cargo be safely landed. If the cargo is sunk for concealment, a deduction is made for the expenses of the recovery unless the crew recover it themselves, which they generally do. If the cargo be thrown over in deep water and irrecoverably lost they receive no compensation whatever for their risk and trouble. The third is the smuggling companies, consisting chiefly of the farmers in the neighbourhood who provide the beach-parties to receive and run the cargo when it is landed, and also bear the whole responsibility after the tubs are on the beach. There may be other occasional arrangements, but the above mentioned are the most used. The locality and other circumstances may sometimes render it expedient to combine the several interests and to allow the risk to be shared in certain proportions, until the ultimate safety of the cargo shall have been secured.

It has been asserted, and, I think, with truth, that if one cargo in three is landed, the smuggling companies are not losers. The price of a tub at Cherbourg is 7/6, the freight per tub about eight shillings, and the expense of running it after landing about six shillings . . .

Your Lordship will observe that in the above arrangements the smuggling companies are always the least sufferers in case of failure, the profits of the parties employed by them being neither so sure nor so great as has been imagined. The men employed by the companies to sail in the vessels are not very numerous, with the exception of the Beer men who work at the bottom of West Bay in smallish vessels. I have seldom boarded a smuggler in ballast on any part of the coast herein laid down, (excepting the Isle of Wight), without finding that most if not all the crew were composed of Portland or Weymouth men. We usually found the stranger on board, and whenever we could ascertain what part of the coast he came from we had no doubt that the boat sailed in that direction, this man being put on board on account of his perfect acquaintance with the proper landing-place for the tub-boat.

I now proceed to state the measures at present resorted to by the Revenue cruisers employed in the prevention of the contraband trade. These vessels are more at anchor than at sea, and when under weigh are seldom out of sight of the English coast. Their boats are left in shore where the vessel may be; sometimes a boat is left for weeks or months at a station many miles distant from the cruising-ground of the vessel. As an instance: the *Greyhound* was never out of Portland Roads unless for a few hours, and very often got under weigh with three or four hands on board, not with an intention of cruising, but that it might appear that they had conformed to the letter of their Printed Instructions. As an instance of the latter, the above stationed at Guernsey had always a detached boat at Weymouth. The *Dove* and *Scourge* always left one at Beer. Your Lordship will be sensible that under this system the expense of the vessels might as well be saved as the Revenue cruising vessels became, in fact, little more than an extra Preventive Service.

By watching the smugglers on market-days and ascertaining where the farmers reside with whom they hold conference; by boarding the vessels when they sail, and observing the wind, weather and age of the moon, it is true that the officers of the Revenue vessels calculate to a great nicety the period and the direction of the vessel's return with their cargoes, but should they intercept them, the smugglers have generally time before the boats can board to sink their cargo, which is all strung together upon a hawser with heavy sinking stones to each end. When these stones are thrown over the side the whole cargo runs out with such rapidity that it requires less than two minutes to sink a cargo of three or four hundred tubs. Indeed, the practice of sinking has become so general on this part of the coast [that] the smuggler prefers doing it whether intercepted or not, as he finds it more safe to work the cargo in small quantities the ensuing night, and it renders him independent of the beach parties, who would otherwise often be collected without being employed in the event of the vessel, by being chased off or other unforeseen circumstances, not arriving at the time appointed. Your Lordship will observe that, throughout the whole transaction, the smugglers have a manifest advantage over the parties employed against them. They have the advantage of being under sail in their vessels and running away from the boats, sinking their cargoes in another direction. They are not kept on the alert for any length of time, being employed only for a few hours, where as the men employed in the Revenue boats have probably been up several nights, and are harrassed with cold and fatigue. The smugglers have also the advantage of silence on their side, and the warning of the noise made by the oars of the parties employed against them; and from their knowledge of the different sinking-grounds and marks on the coast they seldom if ever miss finding their cargoes at the first throw of their creepers.

I have entered into the above details in explanation of the grounds of my confident opinion that not <u>one tub in ten</u>, if so many, falls into the hands of those employed against the smugglers. The great number of tubs, which have been seized by the means at present resorted to, may therefore be considered as <u>evidence of the enormous extent</u> to which the smuggling is carried on than of an <u>effectual check</u> having been put to its continuance. . . .

In proceeding to consider the means of more effectually preventing smuggling than those at present in use, I must beg to refer Your Lordship to a letter written by me to Admiral Whitfield when I paid off His Majesty's Sloop *Rosario*, in which I represented the necessity of employing two vessels of a certain description in West Bay, and expressed an opinion that unless such a measure was resorted to, there never would be any effectual check to the smuggling in that direction.

The situation of Cherbourg is so advantageous to the smugglers from its proximity to the English coast that it will always be in their interest to load at that port, being the only one from which they can start in the evening and load their cargo before break of day, this consideration gives weight to the reasons previously made that every cargo run on the line of coast laid down is shipped at Cherbourg; which port may therefore be considered as the <u>centre</u> from which they all start and the line of coast as the <u>circumference</u>.

I before stated my opinion that the men employed in the smuggling vessels are not very numerous, and the fact of their receiving no remuneration when the cargo is thrown over in deep water. It appears to me, therefore, that the following up [of] a system by which the smugglers would be forced to resort to this expedient or be taken would be the most effectual discouragement to them which could be put in practice. The Officers of the Revenue cruisers are aware of this; but at the same time are aware that by so doing they would have neither prize-money nor the chance of promotion. One Officer only, Mr. . . . of the cutter *Leader* has followed up this system and the smugglers acknowledge that he has done more mischief to them than all the other Revenue cruisers combined.

By forming a cordon round Cherbourg . . . His Majesty's cruisers would have a better chance of falling in with them than when dispersed over coast of a hundred miles in circumference; and having the advantage of superior sailing would oblige them to throw their cargoes overboard to enable them to make their escape. The cruisers would also have a better chance of making a total seizure by a vigilant look-out on the vessel when chased, by seeing her heave her cargo; whereas if close in shore and the vessel and cargo be taken, the crew generally escape in the tub-boat. . . .

It will, therefore, be for Your Lordship's consideration . . . whether it may not be expedient to substitute some other claims of promotion than those at present acknowledged; and to enforce with strictness the execution of a duty which the comfort and emoluments of the Officers will naturally impel them to neglect.

Without trespassing upon Your Lordship's valuable time, I beg to subscribe myself, My Lord, Your Lordship's Most Obedient humble Servant,

Fredk. Marryat.

6th June,
5, Cleveland Row, London.[5]

The 'thin blue line' facing the smugglers had its great figures, as we have seen; but the key figure was always the riding officer of His Majesty's Customs. He was the eyes and ears of the service; he summoned the military to assist him and went into action against the smugglers with them. However, the system was only as good as the weakest link in the chain. The riding officers had been established as early as 1698 to prevent the owling of wool, with 299 being enrolled. In 1734 they were issued with a slim volume entitled *Instructions to Riding Supervisors and Officers of Customs*. In spite of faults in the service and the way the riding officers carried out their duties, they carried on until they handed over their functions to the Coast Guard in 1822.

Originally each riding officer's beat was 10 miles of coast, which he had to patrol by day and night, riding a horse which he had to buy out of his own purse; and he was expected to prevent the smugglers from running their contraband, from which he gained his name, or one of the more polite appellations: 'Preventer'. The riding officer had to rummage ships when they came into ports in his area, and he had to search inland places where he suspected contraband had been hidden. In addition he had to gather intelligence all the time. After each duty the riding officer had to fill in his journal with every detail which he believed would be of interest to his masters, the commissioners of Customs in London.

In 1814 the main Customs House at Billingsgate in London was burned to the ground and all records were destroyed. However, during the Second World War the journal of Chief Riding Officer of Customs Abraham Pike was discovered among family papers in Christchurch, the little Hampshire port where he was based. The journal only covers the years 1803 and 1804, but it is one of the most valuable documents in the whole history of the Revenue service because of its rarity, most other journals having perished in the fire at Billingsgate in 1814.

On the left-hand page Pike had to fill in details of the time and duration of his patrols, where he went, and what the wind and weather were doing; while on the right-hand page he had to report in accordance with the following printed instructions:

Transactions and Observations: particularly what Officers met, and where; what information he receives of goods run, or intended to be run; and what methods he took to prevent the same; what seizures made; what ships he observed on the coast, and which way they sail; and what notice of such ships he gave to the next Officer; what signals he observed from the Commander of the Cutter; and also whatever happens in the day, evening or night that may be fit for the Commissioners' knowledge.

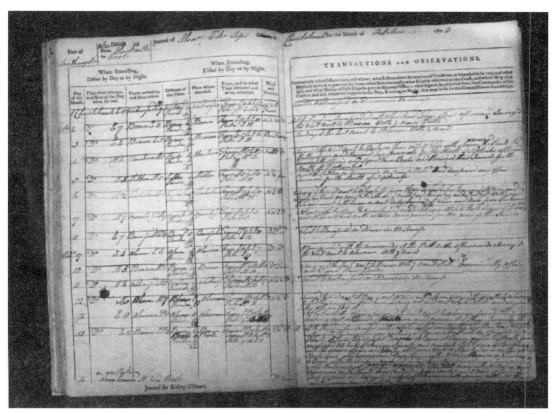

The journal of Abraham Pike, chief riding officer of Customs at
Christchurch

Each area had a supervisor of riding officers with about six riding
officers under him to cover what was called a port district. The
supervisor had over him the Collector of the Customs district, and acted
as coast waiter, in which capacity he searched ships when he suspected
contraband was being carried either in or under perfectly legitimate
cargo.

Abraham Pike's beat stretched from that notorious nest of smugglers
Hurst Castle in the east to the port of Poole in the west, and at the end
of a long ride he had to fill in his report in this book according to the
requirements at the top of the page. It is a record of hard, unremitting
toil:

February 1803. Went to Wootton on discoveries. No success. Surveyed the west coast to Flagstaff. From thence to Parkstone. Examined Mr. Wise [a subordinate riding officer] and signed his book and received his Journals for January. In Iford Lane met the Supervisor of Excise and corresponded. Nothing more occurred. Returned.

. . . Went to the Quay [of the port of Christchurch] on Coast Duty: landing of stone from Poole. Surveyed the east coast to Missway. Saw nothing for the Service. Returned. Went to Haven on Coast Duty: landing of stone from Poole and shipping of malt and barley for Portsmouth.

. . . Surveyed the Haven. Saw the 'Bat' Revenue Cutter, in the Road. Nothing more occurred.

May 1803. Corresponded with Mr. Pritchard, Riding Officer of Lymington, and received a letter from my Collector and Comptroller On His Majesty's Service. Communicated it to my Officers afterwards . . .

Set out with Mr. Bacon and a party. Surveyed the west coast to Bourn[-emouth] and found the smugglers had worked and gone off with the Goods. Traced them to Longham and Upper Kinson. Searched several suspected places. No success.

July. Surveyed the west coast to Bourn. Found a small boat on the shore, the *Invisible* of Poole. From thence to Flagstaff and Parkstone. Examined Mr. Wise who informed me there had been a run of some prohibited goods. . . . Set off with my Officers to Kinson on discoveries. No success. From thence surveyed the east coast to Beacon. Found the smugglers looking out: attended the shore and prevented them from landing.

Surveyed the west coast to Boscombe and Bourn. Saw a cutter in the Bay; imagined it to be the 'Bat' Revenue Cutter. At Bourn found the smugglers had worked. . . . Traced them into the country. Searched several suspected places. In a field near Kingston in the Parish of Ringwood found and seized two casks of foreign spirits. Secured it at my residence.

. . . Called on by Mr. Thomas Lambert, Boatman, informing me he saw a boat come in at Boscombe and landing goods. Set out with my Officers and a party [of cavalry]. In the heath near Boscombe seized two waggons and one cart with 250 casks of foreign spirits and tobacco, and one case of playing-cards . . .

January 1804. Surveyed the west coast to Alum Chine. Called on Mr. Wise and found him incapable of his duty. Set out with Messrs. Preston, Jones and Bacon. Surveyed the west coast . . . in company with Captain Griffiths of the Royal Horse Artillery. Later went with Captain Hunt of the South Hampshire Yeoman Cavalry to inspect the west coast. Nothing more occurred.

. . . Set out with Mr. Bacon to Avon Causeway on discoveries. Found the smugglers gone to the west. Thence returned home for a party of the Royal Horse Artillery. Set out and surveyed the west coast to Alum Chine. Met Mr. Wise. Saw a lugger on the shore. Perceived tracks of carriages: traced them into the Heath and seized 236 casks of foreign spirits, seven casks of tobacco, two waggons, one cart, and thirteen horses and harness . . . Secured goods in His Majesty's Warehouse in the Port of Poole. . . . In the Heath saw a fire lighted up at Bourn. We immediately went to the spot. By the time we got there the fire was out. The smugglers began flashing and striking the light, as it appeared to us, by flint . . .

March 1804. Set out with Messrs. Preston and Jones, and a party of the Royal Horse Artillery. Surveyed the east coast to Missway: found the smugglers looking out. Attended the coast and prevented them from landing. Returned and went to the Haven on Coast Duty . . .

Set out with Mr. Preston and Jones to Thornhill on discoveries. No success. Returned, and corresponded with Mr. James Williams, mate of 'The Bat', Cutter . . .

September 1804. Set out with Mr. Preston. Surveyed the east coast to Missway. Nothing occurred. Returned, and set out with Mr. Preston and surveyed the west coast to Boscombe. Saw a boat on the shore and part of the goods and vessel seized by *The Duke of York*, Excise Cutter.

October 1804. Collected my Officers' Journals for the last month. Afterwards set out with Mr. Bacon to the west coast on discoveries. In the Heath we saw a fire lighted up at Bourne. We immediately went to the spot. By the time we got there the fire was out. The smugglers began flashing and striking of light, as it appeared to us, by flint, and stayed all night in different parts of the Heath, and in the cliffs. We attended the coast all night and prevented them from landing. The night being so very dark we saw no person that was on the coast during the night. On my return, informed Mr. Williams, mate of 'The Bat', Cutter, of the above proceedings. Afterwards Mr. Williams called to inform me that the smugglers had worked at the east. Set out with Mr. Bacon and a party; examined the cross-roads through the Forest [the New Forest]. Found the smugglers was [sic] gone towards Missway. At Missway met Mr. Rutter, Sitter of the Boat at Lymington, and his boat's crew, who informed me the smugglers had been flashing at Beacon. I met Mr. How and Mr. Pinchard and informed them the smugglers was looking out at Missway. They informed me the smugglers had worked the preceding night between Beacon and Missway. Attended the coast all night and prevented them from landing.

Abraham Pike's last entry for 1804 reads:

Surveyed the east coast to beacon. Met Mr. Williams, mate of *The Bat*, Cutter, who informed me there had been a run of goods, about three or four hundred casks, supposed from the *Speedwell*, a cutter of about eighty tons burthen, commanded by Captain Froodge of Guernsey; and that Mr. How, Supervisor, and Mr. Pinchard, Riding Officer, had made a small seizure. Met Messrs. Preston and Newman and with them traced the smugglers into the country at Hinton. Searched several suspected places: no success.[7]

The Mr Newman mentioned in that extract from Abraham Pike's journal was Richard Newman, a very keen riding officer, who in 1799 conceived a novel way of trapping smugglers handling freshly-landed contraband while it was still on the beach, thereby ensuring conviction in court. When one day he had intelligence that a run was due to be made on the beach near Christchurch, in fact not far from the site of the Battle of Mudeford in 1784, he took several of his fellow officers down to the beach upon which the goods were to be landed. There he ordered them to dig themselves shallow 'gun-pits' in the sand just above the tide-line. Each pit was at a good distance from the next and from it each officer could lie and watch the sea for the first sign of incoming smugglers. Every man was armed with cutlass, pistols and musket, for Newman meant to make sure of his prey. When each watcher was in his 'grave', as the humorous fellows had dubbed them, Mr Newman made sure they were well camouflaged with a layer of sand and fronds of seaweed. Then he took his place in his own pit and waited for the smugglers.

At last a lugger came in to the beach, even though there was no landing-party to greet it. Could it have been that the local people had seen what Mr Newman and his men were doing and the smugglers had been warned to stay away from the beach? The lugger's crew came ashore in their tub-boats and stacked their cargo of brandy-kegs on the beach before the Revenue men's very eyes. Not wishing to be caught red-handed the sailors rowed back to their ship and left the bay. Newman had held his fire, for it was the local land-smugglers he was after. He had not long to wait: soon the lander appeared with his crew, and they began loading the kegs into their carts and on to their tubmen's shoulders. Newman waited until they were absorbed in their task and then blew his whistle, at which his men staggered to their frozen feet and gave the smugglers the fright of their lives. They fled, leaving most of the kegs on the beach. Richard Newman was not pleased, for he and his men had only a number of barrels to show for their long nights spent in cold 'graves', and no live smugglers under arrest in their hands. This young, keen officer was to die prematurely as a result of illness contracted on duty in foul weather over a long period, an example of one of the few laudable riding officers in the war against the smugglers.[8]

In practice the job of the riding officer was so badly rewarded and so demanding that there were never enough recruits for the service. By the very nature of the organization, the riding officer was little more than an observer and reporter of the crime of smuggling. In 1783 a senior Customs officer wrote:

> The Riding men are of very little service, though a great burden to the Revenue; and of late years Parliamentary interest has recommended apothecaries, brewers and other tradesmen to these employments, who never ride out but when their own occupations require it, and

fabricate Journals for the rest of the time. And it is generally reported that many of them are the relations of, and even that some of them are agents of, and collectors for, the smugglers, keeping them informed of all they want to know. . . . They are not resolute enough to prove any serious obstacle to large bodies of armed smugglers.

The average age of riding officers was calculated to be sixty, hardly a time of life when the demands of constant riding in all weathers and over all terrains could be met. Most of them did not even know enough about horsemanship to buy themselves reliable mounts: one had his animal die under him while out on patrol; another horse turned out to be so vicious to its new master that it had to be sold as soon as purchased; while yet another, which was bought on the highest recommendation, turned out to be completely blind! Drunkenness was rife among the riding officers, and this in an age of heavy drinking: one Dorset officer was last seen urging his horse into the surf and heard shouting that he intended to ride through the waves along the beach for several miles!

The success of the Landguard depended entirely on the efficiency of it, riding officers as horsemen, so it was no wonder that it was almost useless. The lapse of time between seeing smugglers running goods, and mustering sufficient force to stop them and seize the contraband, usually gave the miscreants time to get away, even when they were using lumbering farm carts for their transport. This was compounded by the attitudes and actions of the detachments of dragoons stationed along the coast for the specific purpose of assisting the riding officers against the smugglers. The dragoon troopers disliked the anti-smuggling duty because they were ordered to fight Englishmen of their own class; they often turned out at night and in the foulest weather, the smugglers' favourite, on dark nights over terrain they did not know, and all this miles away from their own parts of the country: coastal regiments were never used in their own areas for fear of family connections with the men they had to pursue. Above all, the soldiers knew that the smugglers would fight ferociously if they managed to corner them, as shown in the Battle of Hook's Wood, described in Chapter One. All this for only twopence a day. Sending dragoons to catch 'free traders' said someone, was like 'setting elephants to catch eels'. In addition there was the systematic bribing of the soldiers by the smugglers, who would leave a few kegs of spirits, even packets of tea, at the barracks, usually for the attention of the unit's sergeant-major or corporal-of-horse. Worst of all, in the matter of reward, was the system of awarding the prize-money resulting from seizures of contraband, horses and waggons, which was divided within the detachment strictly according to rank, as was the custom in the Royal Navy, of course. This meant that the senior officer got the lion's share simply for staying snug and warm in bed while the troopers were out chasing 'Will o' the Wisps'; and even if there was any for them, it could take as long as three years to come through. Everyone knew this, so where was the incentive?

The riding officer of Customs was, therefore, on his own, neither part of the Army nor Navy, scorned by those very services for that very fact, when he was supposed to work in the closest cooperation with them in this civil warfare. He was loathed by the population, most of whom were smugglers anyway or in sympathy with them, and if he were zealous he could end up dead. As early as 1717 Riding Officer Reeves was killed by the Mayfield Gang in Sussex, the smuggler indicted for the felony being acquitted by his friendly neighbourhood court.[9] And in the late 1780s Riding Officer Bursey of Milford in Hampshire was roused from his bed by two men who told him they would show him a newly-discovered dump of contraband in a nearby barn. As he knew the men he trustingly stepped out of his house, only to be viciously attacked and killed, left on his own threshold to be found by his wife and child the next morning. The authorities assumed Bursey must have been instrumental in setting up a recent ambush of smugglers which had led to a pitched battle on Milford Green.

Even when they managed to kill smugglers who were attacking them, the riding officers could not win: after such an incident in the notorious county of Kent several of the king's officers were taken to court, accused of murder and found guilty. The riding officers were always advised to tackle their enemies only when they had sufficient military assistance at their disposal. But while some commanding officers turned out their men when requested by the riding officers, others went by the book and insisted that the Revenue man's request went through the War Office in London. However, even when they had the soldiers with them when heading for a confrontation with smugglers, few riding officers knew how to deploy the soldiers and use them to their best advantage. Very often the soldiers found that they had been called out too late by their local riding officer and that the smugglers were miles away and out of danger by the time they were in pursuit. There were, in fact, several cases of officers asking dragoons not to attack the smugglers as it would only upset them and make them take revenge on the Revenue men at a later date.

As for the dragoons, or the Royal Horse Artillery, as the case may have been, their sympathies usually lay with the smugglers and they were known to have helped themselves to contraband that they had seized and taken back to their quarters for their own use. A zealous Plymouth Customs officer once asked to search the storeroom in an officers' mess, as he suspected that it housed illegally imported goods. The commanding officer of the unit promptly ordered the sentry on guard over the storeroom to give the preventive officer a few inches of his bayonet if he dared to attempt to enter the room in question.

It is little wonder that so many of the riding officers opted for the easy life. Soon after he took up residence, the newly appointed preventer would have realized that his house was under constant surveillance by the smugglers. They would have his daily routine noted so that they could arrange their affairs without impinging upon his comings and goings. If the riding officer changed his patterns of patrol, it was a simple matter to send him false intelligence to make him race off to one end of his beat while the smugglers were landing their goods at the other. The average riding officer had little to lose, and a great deal to gain, by ignoring any conscience he might have and turning a blind eye to what was going on in the community in which he found himself. As the case of Mr Bursey of Milford well shows, the riding officer was often in great physical danger if he showed a combative spirit and any intention of doing his duty. If he displeased the smugglers, the best he could hope for was to be tied up and imprisoned in a cellar until a run was over; or, if he were really troublesome, he could well be grabbed, shipped across to France in a smuggling vessel and dumped on foreign soil in his king's uniform. In peacetime this could mean no more than a few uncomfortable hours in the cells of the local gendarmerie, but in time of war it meant capture as a belligerent, a long stay in a French gaol, or death at the hands of his discoverers or the muskets of a French firing-squad.

CHAPTER THREE

COMMODITIES

What did the smugglers smuggle? The short answer is anything upon which the government had laid a high or fairly high duty. In the Middle Ages it was mainly wool, and that was smuggled *out* of the country by the 'owlers'. But in the age of Queen Elizabeth I it was not a question of duty which motivated the biggest English smugglers; rather the opposite. They smuggled English cannons made by the ironmasters of the Weald of Kent over to France, down through Italy and across the Mediterranean Sea to Spain. So it was that, thanks to the smugglers, the finest guns used by the galleons of the Armada on the ships of Raleigh and Drake had been made in their very own country. Elizabethan smugglers *did* run an import trade, but again this was not to circumvent paying monetary duty, but because it was totally forbidden for these commodities to be brought into the realm. They were collectively known as 'popish stuff', destined for the underground old religionists who clung to the outlawed Roman Catholic faith: Douai Bibles, crucifixes, religious pictures, statues, relics blessed by the Pope in Rome, and all manner of medallions and amulets forbidden by royal decree. It would be a mistake to think the English smugglers of this period or any other ran these goods out of any other motive than the desire for pure profit, for they were well paid by the Pope's agents, bent on the 'Enterprise of England' and its conversion back to the old religion. The goods came in small but highly profitable amounts, hidden in bales of cloth and boxes of legal commodities.

Customs duties varied considerably throughout the great smuggling period which took off in the early eighteenth century. When duty was high it paid to smuggle; when duties were lowered or abolished by the government the smugglers switched commodities, selecting those which were currently most profitable. By the accession of King George III in 1760 there were some 800 items on which duty had to be paid; but in the next fifty years an enormous 1,300 were added to the list. So, in that golden age, a huge variety of goods were smuggled: lace, kerchiefs, dresses, gloves, silks, satin, calico, velvet, ribbon, brocade, snuff (both plain and scented), straw hats, dried fruits, tobacco, whisky, brandy, gin, wine, cordials, tea, chocolate, coffee, sugar, spices, dice, playing-cards, soap, coconuts, embroideries, precious metals, pearls, salt, pepper, sealing-wax, fine timbers for furniture, books of certain sorts, hair-powder, starch, vinegar, wire and coffin-nails. Without the work of the smugglers those commodities which were becoming necessities in everyday life would not have been available to ordinary people, and the upper classes would certainly not have had their luxuries.

Tea had arrived in Britain around 1657, Samuel Pepys drinking it for the first time on 25 September 1660, and by 1730 the trade was big business between China and Europe. By 1750 it was a national staple, rivalling beer and ale, and being drunk at all meals with plenty of smuggled sugar. However, the cheapest legal tea in the shops cost about 7s. a pound, almost a week's wages for a labouring man, and in the comfortable houses of the middle and upper classes the ornate, wooden tea-caddy was lockable, the sort of article we see in stately homes to this day. Smuggled tea, though, was a mere 2s. a pound; the other 5s. was customs duty, imposed as early as 1680.

Tea-smuggling started way down the Channel: as the great East India Company's ships paused to pick up their pilots from the Isles of Scilly they started selling tea, as well as other wares, over the side to boats pulling out from the isles, Cornwall and Devon. Tea was always the most profitable commodity because its value was so high in proportion to its bulk. The government realized this and slashed the duty on it (in 1745, for instance), but it could not resist reinstating such a tempting source of revenue. By 1780 two-thirds of the tea being drunk in Britain was smuggled, and Mr Twining lead the tea-merchants lobbying Parliament to lower the duty, put more effort into stopping the smuggling, and end the adulteration of tea with leaves plucked from English hedgerows.[1]

However, tea was too much of a good thing for the smugglers to lay off, and not just because of its huge value: sewn into oilskin bags by the smugglers' counterparts across the Channel, it was light, very easy to handle, impossible to damage and simple to hide. Tea could even be

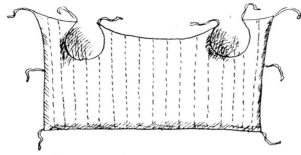

Eighteen Rows in the above Waistcoat or Stays, well stuff'd with Tea, weighing about 8 lbs.

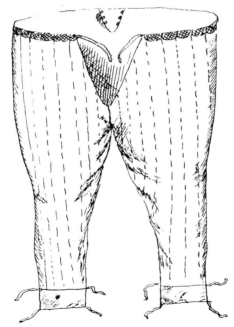

The above worn is a pair of Drawers, made of Stout Cotton, secured with strong drawing Strings, stuff'd with Tea, and weighing about 16 lbs.

Tea smugglers' underclothes (HM Customs & Excise)

smuggled by pedestrians: canvas drawers, coats and waistcoats were specially made for the 'duffers', as these specialist smugglers were called, with lots of pockets containing tea, up to about 100 lb in weight sometimes. With dogged relentlessness they would plod from East Anglia and the marshes of Essex into London, the great tea-capital of the world, both legal and illegal. Dr Johnson may have called the smuggler 'a wretch', but he confessed elsewhere that he himself was '. . . a hardened and shameless tea-drinker, who has for twenty years diluted his meals with only the infusion of this fascinating plant; whose kettle has scarcely time to cool; who with tea amuses the evening, with tea solaces the midnight, and with tea welcomes the morning'.[2] Perhaps he drew a distinction between smugglers and duffers.

The tea smuggled into London was not just for the British: much of it was taken from the London depots, loaded into fishing-boats a mile down the River Thames below Gravesend and sailed across to Rotterdam, to such huge effect that this traffic threatened to make a mockery of any bonding system. The problem of the London smugglers grew so acute that the government decided they would have to use the crack cavalry regiments quartered in the capital, but, as one writer put it, the smugglers 'come into London without fear, knowing the Officers have no horse-soldiers to oppose them with'. The Westminster Excise officers decided they had had enough of the smugglers' pony-trains passing through their streets, near to the seat of government itself, at the dead of night. They were usually making for their headquarters in Stockwell in Lambeth, where they had a huge set of receiving-depots from which the London shop-keepers bought their contraband tea and other goods. It was while searching a Stockwell house that a Revenue officer found a rare smugglers' invoice in a pile of oilskin teabags. It ran: 'Mr. A.B., Dr. to Woking: 200 bags of tea: £200'. The king's officers were dying to raid Stockwell but they hesitated time and again, knowing that the populace would oppose them and disperse the contraband to their houses, stables, gardens and purpose-built cellars. One law-abiding resident found a load of teabags had been dumped in his garden by night, but he dared not report it for he knew the smugglers would kill him or, at the very least, burn his house to the ground.

However, in 1768 the officers seized 500 lb of tea in a guarded dump in a field in Stockwell. The smugglers whistled for help and immediately sixty men charged out of the surrounding houses and went for the king's men with stones and bricks and drove them off. After that officers were regularly set on if they became too inquisitive, and were not safe after dark even in large groups. Also, the local residents were always keen to help their heroes, the smugglers. One quiet May evening two small-time smugglers landed a batch of teabags right on the Thames Embankment, but the watch spotted them and gave chase. The smugglers dropped their load in Dirty Lane just off the Strand. The watch impounded it and lodged it in the Round House in Covent Garden, sending for a Customs officer to make the official seizure in the king's name. But by the time he arrived the smugglers had roused their mates, and when he tried to leave with the consignment a huge mob had surrounded the Round House determined to prevent him going off with their tea. The leaders of the mob were, apparently, the local constable and the parish beadle.[3]

It was in this period that the utter reliability and acceptability of the smuggler, particularly the tea-bringer, was immortalized by Parson Woodforde in his famous diary: '29th March, 1777: . . . Andrews the Smuggler brought me this night about eleven o'clock a bag of Hysson tea, six pounds weight. He frightened us a little by whistling under the parlour window just as we were going to bed. I gave him some Geneva [gin] and paid him for the tea at ten and sixpence per pound.' On 27 May 1780 he wrote: 'To Richard Andrews for two tubs of gin paid £2.10.0d.' And two years later: 'To Clark Hewitt this evening for a tub of gin which be brought in a basket . . .'[4]

This Geneva or gin was specially distilled for the English smugglers in purpose-built distilleries in Dunkirk and other Channel ports such as Boulogne. In the 1730s Lord Hervey found that in Britain 'Drunkenness of the common people is so universal by the retailing of a liquor called Gin, with which they could get drunk for a groat, that the whole town of London and many towns in the country swarmed with drunken people from morning to night, and were more like a scene of a Bacchanal than the residence of a civil society.'[5] William III is generally discredited with bringing in gin and popularizing it for it was a Dutch favourite, and got its name from *genièvre* meaning 'juniper', from the berries of which tree it is distilled. 'Drunk for a penny, dead drunk for twopence, straw for nothing' was a real inn-and-shop sign and shows how gin was now the ruinous tipple of the lowest classes.

However, it was another spirit brought in by the smugglers which is for ever associated with them in the popular mind. It was Dr Johnson who wrote: 'Claret is the liquor for boys; port for men; he who aspires to be a hero must drink brandy!' But this aqua vitae was good for those who were not feeling heroic at all: everyone knew from way back in the Middle Ages that brandy cured colic, dropsy, paralysis, fever, toothache, gout and a hundred other ailments, either taken straight or as the liquor for infusions. It also stimulated the heart, protected against plague, and kept those who drank it regularly ever young. In the fighting services it was not only the giver of Dutch courage, but it was the prime antiseptic, anaesthetic and warmer of bodies rescued from icy seas. It preserved the body after death too, as Nelson's last voyage home as a corpse steeped in a huge tun of brandy testifies. Once the body was taken out, the liquor which was left fetched the highest prices of any liquid in the history of Britain. Johnson had been right once again.

The brandy or cognac, known as 'Cousin Jack' in the smugglers' code of rhyming slang, smuggled in was usually about 80 per cent proof, but the finest cognac which came in was nearly pure spirit at around 93 per cent. It was a clear liquid when it arrived, but the British liked their brandy honey-coloured: a number of French merchants supplied free caramel to tint it over in Britain, while many smuggling towns preferred to do it themselves with sugar. It is said that in many of these places one could walk out into the evening air and breathe in the balmy perfume from the burnt sugar with which the smugglers' ladies were colouring the cognac their menfolk had just run in. The free-trading buyer would usually pay about 5s. for a gallon of brandy over there, to sell it over here at 25s. (See the assessments made in the letters and reports in the previous chapter.) Customs duty would have put the price up to 32s. Brandy was usually smuggled in a 'half-anker', commonly called a 'keg' or 'tub' and holding around 4½ imperial gallons. The French merchant would sell the brandy in his warehouse in pairs of kegs, custom-made and tied together with rope specially designed for the English smugglers' running methods.

The French cognac suppliers were, naturally, very helpful: the Calais distillers fitted out ten brandy-carrying vessels, which would meet English smugglers in mid-Channel and sell as much drink to them as they could in the shortest possible time. The first captain to sell his cargo collected the money the others had made up to that point and then raced back to Calais for another load of kegs. The French crews were paid by commission, so this made them speedy; but if their cargoes were seized they got no payment at all.

When the wars against the French started in 1793 the importation of all French products was forbidden. The English smugglers were delighted for they had no sense of patriotism where money was in the offing.

'East India goods', brought in by the huge ships of that company, comprised such articles as silks, spices and piece-goods, and were not only sold over the side as the ships sailed up the English Channel, but also in the ports once they were riding at anchor. In the Solent the far-travelled captains would invite the drapers of the cities of Southampton and Portsmouth to view their silks and calicoes before they went into the Customs houses. As early as 1633 the *Royal James* reached the Thames and had her cargo listed as being worth £796, rather different from the £58,000 estimate which had been placed upon her spices when she had set off on her long voyage in the Far East. The Customs service codified strict rules which they vainly tried to apply to these East India men, but their crews managed to go on smuggling as ever.[6]

A ship of the East India Company. When entering the English Channel it was ships such as these that did brisk trade with the smugglers over their sides, well before they came under the eyes of the King's ships which escorted them into the great ports of the kingdom

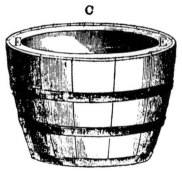

A.—Section of Cask in its original state.

B.—Section of half the Cask cut from head to head.

C.—Section of Cask cut transversely.

D.—The Tin lining.

E.—The space between the Tin lining and the Cask in which the Segars were secreted.

Barrels for smuggling cigars (HM Customs & Excise)

Tobacco had always been smuggled, except for the times when duty on it had been suddenly lowered. After 1800 it became a better bet even than tea, on which duty had been drastically cut. Whenever tobacco was seized by the Revenue officers it was publicly burned, surrounded by cordons of soldiers, and watched by furious local onlookers. It had been King James I's hatred of tobacco which had originally made it worth smuggling, for he had imposed a very high Customs duty on it as the only way to prevent the majority from enjoying it. The Spaniards started taking tobacco into the Channel Islands and from there it was smuggled into England. Then the Royal Navy entered the game, selling tobacco and also spirits, illegally. Tobacco continued as a strong favourite with the smugglers right up into the second half of the nineteenth century. Cigars were the most popular form, and they came into the country hidden in barrels, in batches of toys from the Continent, dangling inside ladies' crinolines, and stuffed inside muffs.

Clarissa was a smugglers' doll which was brought across from France by the smugglers who specialized in ladies' dresses. Clarissa would be wearing, in miniature, the latest Paris fashions, right down to underwear, and the ladies in the great houses in which she was entertained would choose the items they liked best. The smugglers would bring the latest styles over from France on their next trip. This activity continued even in wartime.

CHAPTER FOUR

RUNNING

For smuggling to have threatened the very survival of the country, as many politicians believed it did, it must have been a traffic of enormous proportions, directed by men of great commercial and administrative skill. In 1781 the outraged Lord Pembroke demanded in a ringing sentence: 'Will Washington take America or the smugglers England first?'

We know very little of the men who directed this illicit trade year in and year out, switching from commodities suddenly no longer profitable to others on which duty had been suddenly raised or imposed; buying bigger and faster ships in which to outsail the enemy, both Revenue and Royal Navy; and constantly crewing these vessels with some of the finest seamen in the world. The directors of the free trade kept themselves out of the limelight for the most part, and left no written records of their business behind; but several of them were millionaires by today's standards, and most enjoyed the finest lifestyles.

Each run of contraband began with the venturer, a name which had for centuries been used by perfectly respectable sea-merchants, and it was he who collected through his agent (the bagman) the sum of money needed for the purchase of the goods on the other side of the Channel. The bagman's task was to go around the locality collecting the shares in the enterprise, after which he would take the bag across the Channel in the smuggling vessel. Once in the warehouse run specially for the smugglers he would do the shopping from the list of the shareholders' requirements. The venturer's accounts were kept by the 'quill-driver', often the parish clerk or the village schoolmaster. We know nothing of his accounting for naturally no ledger or list has survived.

The fourth man of importance in a run was the captain of the smuggling ship. He had to enjoy the full confidence of the venturer, whether he was hired or directly employed by the organization. The captain had to know every inch of the English coast, or at least the area where he landed the goods, like the back of his hand; he also had to know the winds, the tides and the currents, as well as every seamark ashore by which to reckon his landfalls. The captain had to be a supremely efficient navigator, able to find a beach on a pitch-dark night and in the foulest weather. It was skills such as these which made smuggling captains very welcome in the Royal Navy, whether they joined voluntarily (not a very likely possibility), were impressed by the press-gang or were sentenced to service in the king's ships once caught and convicted of smuggling in court. Such men had their service numbers prefixed by the letters 'C.P.' which signified that they had been handed over to the service by the 'Civil Powers'. Members of smuggling crews similarly enlisted in the Royal Navy were equally welcome as they were usually prime, seasoned seamen, and suitable for promotion to petty officer after distinguishing themselves in action. Even the worst smugglers were better than the usual prizes collected for the service by the press-gangs. Some smuggling captains such as Tom Johnstone, the Hampshire smuggler, were used by the Admiralty as pilots in wartime enterprises across the Channel. Others were both venturer and captain combined because they owned their own vessels.

Once the money was collected in the bag, the bagman was taken across the water by the captain, the landing-place and time having been agreed with the venturer. The Channel Islands, Roscoff, Cherbourg, Dunkirk, Boulogne or some port in the Low Countries would be reached and here the huge depots run almost exclusively for the English smugglers would be used for the choosing of the various commodities ordered by the venturer. Spirit-kegs already roped in pairs, tea in waterproof packets and tobacco, well compressed to take up as little space as possible, would be carefully stowed in the vessel under the direction of the captain. Later in the period this process was particularly tricky and secret compartments had to be built into the ships to fool the keen rummaging crews of the coastal blockade and, later, the Coast Guard.

At sea it was always a matter of trying to avoid interception by the king's ships if possible, but if they pursued a smuggling vessel they were always given a good run for their money and more cargoes got through than did not. The venturers always said that even if they lost one cargo in three they were still making a profit. Coming into the agreed beach at the agreed time, the 'spot', as it was called, needed a good 'spotsman', something all successful smuggling captains had to be. Having arrived at the right place, the captain would send a blue flash by lantern to the shore, to be answered by the 'flink' or flash from the lookout of the waiting beach-party. To ensure that it could only be seen at sea and not by any watcher either way along the coast, this signal was made by a spout lantern, specially made for the smugglers by the local blacksmith. The flink told the captain that 'the coast was clear', a smuggling expression that has passed into our language.

Once the signal had been seen, the smuggler would drive into the shore and anchor as close as he dared, taking wind, tide and current into account. He dropped a tub-boat into the water which usually took in the tub-line, the end of which was given to a member of the beach-party in the surf. He would then haul the line in, and so the pairs of kegs, tied to it at intervals before the voyage started, would arrive in waiting hands and be severed from the line by the smugglers' knives. Each roped pair would be flung over the

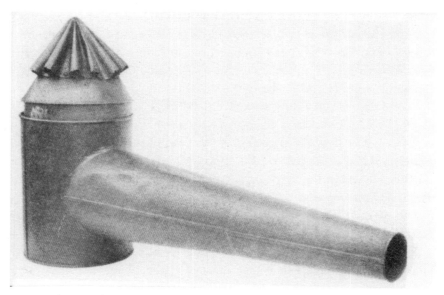

The spout lantern, made specially for smugglers, was held in the crook of the arm and the aperture was covered by the other hand. The flash or 'flink' to the smuggling ship coming into the shore was made by briefly removing this hand from the hole

shoulders of the waiting tubman, who would then get off the beach as quickly as possible. Other packages, such as larger barrels, bales and even boxes, would be brought ashore and put on ponies or into farm-waggons, which would start the long journey inland as quickly as possible.

The 'lander' was not only in charge of the beach-party which received and carried off the smuggled goods, but was also responsible for assembling the men, beasts of burden and draught, and the waggons which transported the goods. The lander was heavily involved in what we today would call logistics. When the king's forces were weak his task was easy, but when attack was likely, because a vigilant lookout had alerted strong anti-smuggling forces, such as the dragoons, it was fraught with problems. Firstly the lander had to select strong and trustworthy men for his beach-party, men who needed the money, and who would be free enough and sober enough to run the goods on the appointed night. He would also have to choose men who knew the country for miles around, men who were loyal to the company or gang which presided over that part of the coast. The lander had to know what goods were going to be run so that he would be able to provide the right numbers of tubmen, ponies, waggons and, if trouble was expected, a sufficiently strong force of 'batmen' to guard the convoy with the holly-bats, the smugglers' infantry. He also had to arrange the men's payment, in both money and goods, and even meals.

The waggons and horses were provided by the farmers of the area: the lander would leave verbal instructions about how many were needed, and the stables would be left unlocked when he needed to collect them. Farmers who were reluctant to help could expect to have their stables and ricks burned down, or worse. Such hard measures were part of the lander's responsibility, and went together with reprisals against anyone foolish enough to act as informer. Farmers who cooperated found their possessions safely returned together with the smuggled goods they had ordered, and payment in kind left in the stables with the tired animals. In many places the farmers supplied rope traces instead of leather, felt horseshoes, and even leather washers for the wheels of their waggons, all in the cause of secrecy and silence.

Above all the lander had to be a genius at timing: having dismissed his forces without alerting the local riding officers of Customs, he had to

The batman: tough and ready to use the steel–tipped
quarter–staff known as the 'bat'

summon them in the same way. Usually he told them to meet in a barn
near the shore, or inside the walls of an ancient earthwork if one was
conveniently situated adjacent to the appointed beach. Once grouped,
the lander's greatest worry was drink: not all smugglers would wait in
the cold without some liquid heating, and tipsy singing was the last thing

'A view near Shoreham, with smugglers landing a cargo'

he wanted. The lander then had to post his lookouts and signallers. Once the cargo had started to come ashore the lander had to drive his men to work as swiftly and silently as they could, for this was the part of the run where the smugglers were at their most vulnerable: to be caught in the act of running contraband was just what the king's officers wanted, for they could then get convictions.

The lander was also responsible for detailing to his transporters the directions in which they had to walk or drive, using the names of local roads and paths, and the locations of the places where the contraband had to be off-loaded. These could be anywhere from private gardens, churchyards, churches themselves, tombs, woodsheds, ponds, stables, firewood-heaps, cowsheds, ditches, chimney flues, hollow trees, potato-clamps, fuel-sheds, apple-lofts, haystacks, pigsties, rainwater-butts, culverts, hedgerows and a host of purpose-built hides, many of them brick-lined for dryness and cunningly concealed. It must have been a complex business, done by word of mouth, and probably without anything committed to paper by anyone, least of all the lander himself, for any such document would have been fatally incriminating if found by the king's officers.

'Free Traders', as the smugglers liked to be known, passing along a street where
the villagers wisely 'watch the wall'. If questioned later by the King's men
they may then say with truth that they saw no one passing with contraband

Churches were favourite hiding-places for contraband which had to be
stored until the hue and cry of any search died down, after which the
goods would be taken further inland when the coast was clear. Most
vicars allowed their premises to be used, for they were among the
smugglers' best customers, as Parson Woodforde has shown, and they
were paid in kind for the use of them. There were some exceptions, like
the priest who was asked by his parish clerk whether smuggling was a sin.
When assured that it was, the clerk said: 'Then pity this poor town, sir,
for who is here who has not had a keg?' The smugglers could hardly have
resisted the dry storage afforded by church crypts, and it seems certain
that many of them had tunnels leading into them from rivers and inns in
the towns which they served. However, one vicar turned informer when,
for some reason, the smugglers ceased paying him their rent.

Another was conducting his bishop round his church on a formal
visitation of the small seaside parish. In a corner of the nave they came
upon a pile of brandy-kegs which some of the smuggling parishioners
had had to stash there at short notice when hard pressed. The vicar
glanced at his bishop to see if he had noticed; but the great prelate
walked on, looking straight ahead, saying not a word. Another vicar,
hurrying into the church to take a service, was stopped by a smuggler
who said the service would have to be cancelled. When asked why, the

Studland church, Dorset. The door just beneath the roof
is the entrance to the loft over the chancel, which has a
narrow window facing the sea used for signalling by
smugglers; they used the roof for storage

parishioner replied that his pulpit was full of tea and his vestry full of
kegs. The parson understood completely, for he had seen the Customs
officers searching as he had entered the church.[1]

The smugglers were naturally very keen to keep all snoopers away
from the churches they were using, and the revival, invention and
spreading of ghost stories were part and parcel of their running
technique. In places like castles, which they used as depots, similar scare
stories abounded, the most famous being the ghostly drummer of
Herstmonceux Castle in Sussex, who scared off innumerable locals who
might have seen what the smugglers did not wish them to see.

The most famous ruse used by smugglers to frighten off prying eyes was the
ghostly drummer who walked the south gallery of Herstmonceux Castle,
beating his drum and glowing with phosphorous paint to frighten intruders
away from the contraband which was hidden in the ruins

Tunnels that were used are often said to have run for several miles.
Although many people find it impossible to believe that anyone would
have gone to all the trouble of constructing them, certainly for such
distances, the smuggling directors envisaged smuggling continuing for
many years, so why not invest money and labour in these tunnels? Many
sewers were used, of course, but quite how the smugglers managed in
the confined space we do not know. Nevertheless, it is a matter of
recorded fact that in the port of Poole legitimate ships bringing in
contraband under cover of their proper cargo unloaded it into tunnels
which ran from holes in the quay to inns on the other side of the
loading area. The tunnels were too small for a smuggler to go through
himself, so the goods were hauled ashore by a system of lines running
through the tunnels, a method which must have been used in many
south coast ports. Tunnels were not an invention of the smugglers: many
an old house, castle and monastery had them too, and the smugglers
would have made use of them with alacrity.

Apart from the inns, houses and shops to which the smugglers
delivered their contraband, there were the open-air markets in remote,
easily guarded locations where customers came from many miles around
on fixed days to buy what the smugglers had on offer: Ridley Wood in

the New Forest, Tidpit Down near Martin in Hampshire, and Smugglers' Mead near Blandford in Dorset. It would seem, therefore, that the contrabandists were never left with goods unsold: everything was turned to profit in the free trade.

The smugglers had other permanent features which they used like the tunnels. It seems that their paths over open country may have been marked every few hundred yards or so by pine trees planted by the local smuggling directors, while in the older villages in the south it is possible to see small windows in the ends of houses which give a clear view of the street, as though they were meant for watching the approach of the smugglers. By the same token, walls of courtyards abutting on houses along village streets sometimes have small hatchways with doors, cut at about chest height, the probable delivery-hole for the smugglers when they called on customers with a standing order.

In Devon, also, bottle-ends can still be seen embedded in the plaster of some cottages, though whether these indicated regular customers or were safe houses for smugglers is not certain.

On a much larger scale were the smugglers' towers, which today are usually dismissed as being follies or eye-catching features built by landowners to enhance the interest of their estates. One such edifice stands on the edge of Kimmeridge Bay in Dorset and was built in 1800 by a parson, the Revd John Clavel, who happened to be the local squire, his seat being the impressive Smedmore House nearby. Some people believed it was an observatory from which the squire could view the heavens, others that it was another folly; others still stated flatly that it was a lookout-post and signal tower for the Kimmeridge Bay free traders, in whose company the Revd Clavel must have been an important member. Certainly Clavel's Hard, which still appears on the Ordnance Survey map, was constructed in the rocks as a safe and capacious landing-place. Another function of the tower was also, of course, to act as a seamark for ships coming into Clavel's Hard.

A yet larger tower, still dismissed by some as a grand folly, is Luttrell's Tower, some miles to the east at Eaglehurst in Hampshire. This magnificent building, now owned by the Landmark Trust, stands on a 30 ft cliff and is 110 ft high. Its three storeys are linked by a spiral staircase going right up to the battlemented roof, from where there are magnificent views over Southampton Water, Spithead, Portsmouth, the

Solent and the Isle of Wight, for the slim tower on top of the rooms extends another 25 ft. This amazing building was the achievement of one Temple Simon Luttrell, and was constructed between the years 1730 and 1750. Its builder was of an ancient Irish family, and although it is not certain when he was born, it is widely held that he died in a prison in France in the year 1803. It is also believed that Luttrell was a specialist smuggler who supplied the royal family and the aristocracy with the finest French wines and cognacs. The enormous height of his custom-built tower would have enabled signallers to indicate to Luttrell's smuggling vessels where to land their fine cargoes, for from its summit the lookouts would have seen both sea and land, with the riding officers under constant surveillance. If the goods were run ashore directly under the great tower they could be brought into storage in the basement through the tunnel running from there to the beach.

The greatest nuisance experienced by the English smugglers was pursuit by riding officers and their henchmen, the dragoons. A delaying tactic involved the smugglers' lantern-bearer detaching himself from the main party and striking off in another direction, leading the king's men astray and hopefully 'thorough bush, thorough briar'[2] so that they got properly bogged down. This *ignis fatuus* might even allow himself to be captured if the chase was particularly hot.

There were cases of smugglers landing kegs on which duty had, in fact, been paid, and, when seized by the Customs, they brought actions for wrongful seizure of custom-paid goods. The local jury would always award large damages to their friends the smugglers. Rumour was also used to misinform the Revenue: in 1730 the London smugglers spread the word that they were going to send a large load across the River Thames by the Lambeth ferry; in fact they used the Battersea ferry, the Customs men waiting in vain for them, and got clean away with their consignment.

Smuggling was rife in the Royal Navy: the tars went for gold and silver coins wherever they docked, building up goodly stocks in their sea-chests. When suspicious rummagers from the port Customs asked for permission to search His Majesty's ships the captains invariably refused. In 1767 HMS *Active* anchored in Spithead on returning from the West Indian station where her crew had stocked up with finest Jamaican rum; before the gaugers could get aboard, the bluejackets signalled a Royal Navy barge to come alongside from the dockyard of Portsmouth, loaded

Luttrell's Tower, Eaglehurst, near Calshot in Hampshire

the casks at dead of night and sent the barge back. The local Revenue cutter challenged the barge and called upon it to heave to, its boarding-party being foiled by the king's sailors, who pushed most of the preventers into the water with their oars. Once disengaged, the rum-laden barge was rowed swiftly into the Royal Navy dockyard where no Customs craft were allowed to follow.[3]

Smugglers by an anonymous artist, published in 1807 (HM Customs & Excise)

The vessels used by the English smugglers ranged from small rowing-boats, through the so-called 'pilot-gigs' of the Isles of Scilly, to the luggers and cutters of the highly active period of smuggling, and were usually built specially for their illegal work. They were, moreover, sailed by the most skilful seamen the country had ever produced, men who not only knew the management of their craft but also every current, tide and hazard they might meet, as well as each cove, bay, beach and island along the complicated English coast. As the smuggling war progressed these seamen grew steadily in skill and cunning, not only in boat management but also in the ingenuity needed, particularly in the scientific age, to conceal their contraband in more and more hiding-places.

A Customs cutter chasing a smuggling lugger, and flying the required
pennant to indicate to other vessels she was in lawful pursuit (HM Customs
& Excise)

At the beginning of the period the smugglers' favourite ship was the
lugger, which could be anything from 50 to 300 tons in displacement.
The largest of these exceptionally handy vessels were capable of carrying
up to something like 3,000 half-ankers of spirits, together with, if
necessary, around 12 tons of tea to top up the enormous cargo. As the
struggle with the forces of the Crown grew progressively more desperate
and complicated, these luggers were fitted with more and more guns,
several of the larger luggers having as many as fifteen fourteen-pounder
cannon mounted on their capacious decks. It was this type of smuggling
craft that William Arnold, the new Collector of Customs on the Isle of
Wight in Hampshire, warned his masters on the Board of Customs
about in his reports on the situation which he found when he took up
his appointment in the year 1777.

The lugsail rig enabled these ships to run very close to the wind, and to claw in and out of narrow inlets where their shallow draught was a huge advantage, for it enabled them to get very close to the shore onto which their cargoes had to be unloaded with the greatest possible speed.

The lugger needed a very shallow keel because her bottom was very flat, her beam very broad and her masts quite short. It was when they were being pursued by the cutters of the Royal Navy and the Revenue service that these qualities were really appreciated by the smugglers, for with the deep keels of the king's ships there was no possibility of closing with the enemy in such shallow waters. In addition, the lugger was by no means a slow vessel for its great sails, in the lugsail configuration, gave it great wind-catching abilities. Perhaps the most surprising fact about the lugger was that it was not an English but a French invention, and it made the sea passage between the land of its birth and England in amazingly short times, eight hours sometimes being quoted as the record for the distance at the Channel's widest point.

So roomy were the larger luggers that when the smugglers sailed in convoy they were able to carry companies of 'smugglers' marines', whose job was to repel boarders if a chase resulted in a king's ship getting alongside for boarding. When the scientific age was ushered in after the defeat of Napoleon at the Battle of Waterloo in 1815, the smuggling luggers were large enough to accept plenty of false compartments and

Invented by the French who named it the 'Chasse Marée', it was known by
the English smugglers as the lugger

lower decks, which became essential for the hiding of contraband, because the Coast Guard was a far more thorough rummager than the old style Revenue men had ever been.

The smugglers saw how fast the enemy's cutters were when in hot pursuit, and they soon decided that they must equip themselves with this high-speed ship too. Sloop-rigged on a single mast, with the running bowsprit which, appearing to cut through the water, gave the type its name of 'cutter', it had a very deep keel to compensate for the leverage imparted to the ship by the huge spread of sails needed to give it its great speed. A cutter could be anything up to 150 tons, and many carried a dozen or more guns; but the mixture of square and jib sails could give the ship a top speed through the water of just over 12 knots. Of course, this deep keel kept it out of shallow waters, but the high speed and considerable capacity for cargo meant that a newly launched cutter was soon paying its way. One of the most famous of the breed was the *Ranger*, built at Cawsand in Cornwall, with a hundred-strong crew and twenty-two guns. So formidable was she that she was able to land her goods in Torbay in daylight, and no Revenue cutter dared approach. Another notorious cutter was the *Swift* which could carry 2,000 barrels and 5 tons of tea on each voyage, and in just one year she had paid for her building costs.

Another type of smuggling vessel, purpose-built for the job, was the galley. The best known were made in that notorious smuggling town Deal, in Kent. These had a large lugsail and about five rowing thwarts or seats. They were steered by means of an oar when being rowed, and a rudder when it was under sail. The Deal galley needed an enormous amount of ballast because of its narrow beam, shallow draught and large area of sail; this weight had to be shifted to the weather side at each change of tack. A much faster craft, capable, it is said, of as much as 16 knots, was the clinker-built smuggling yawl. This was double-ended like the Viking drakkars from which they are supposed to have descended, with two masts, a lugsail rig, a length of anything up to 60 ft' and a crew of thirty. For fast passages with contraband such as golden guineas, these must have been ideal.

A similar galley was known as the 'Death' because it was so dangerous to sail. Specifically designed with no cargo-space, it had no need of any, because the cargo was carried in the money-belts round the waists of the

The 'Death' galley: the fast guinea-smuggling craft

rowers: golden guineas being taken across to pay for contraband or, during the French wars, to be sold, each one worth 30s. on the French market. It was very fast, with little keel, and a square sail, and it was made of the cheapest wood for it was regarded as expendable.

When any of these galleys were chased by the Navy or Revenue they simply turned into the eye of the wind and escaped their sail-driven pursuers with great ease. They would make for the nearest beach in shallow water, run into it and be lifted out of the sea by the crew, who would then carry the boat inland and into hiding. The Kent galleys made good use of the treacherous Goodwin Sands, on which they would land when pursued, and be carried by their crews across the sand bar and launched on the other side to escape their pursuers, who could only look helplessly on from the deep water. One cutter captain described the pursuit of a galley by a cutter as 'sending a cow after a hare'.[4]

The Customs cutters were the front-line vessels in the war between the Crown and the smugglers as it went into its most crucial phase in the last quarter of the eighteenth century. Clinker-built of very strong construction, they shipped a tall, stout mast as well as the long bowsprit on which they mounted huge areas of sail for their size. The bowsprit was very nearly the same length as the hull, and was only allowed on Customs vessels, for, by the Act of 1787, bowsprits of more than two-thirds of the hull length were illegal, and rendered the vessel liable to seizure. The Revenue cutters averaged twelve guns as their main armament, with as many swivel-guns as they needed, and the crew of about thirty were heavily armed with personal weapons for boarding. These seamen formed an elite body, well paid, exempt from impressment into the Royal Navy, and with an *esprit de corps* which made them superb crews, enjoying rewards of gratifying size from seizures of smuggling ships. Their captains became the aces of the sea war, in much the same way that fighter pilots were in the two World Wars. They faced the worst of weathers for this was the smugglers' favourite sort; and when they chased and boarded a quarry they could count on being murderously resisted, for their enemies were in the tightest of corners and would fight like demons. Once the French wars started, they faced another enemy.

CHAPTER FIVE

THE SMUGGLERS

To the east of Southampton Water they were generally called 'gangs', but to the west they were usually styled 'companies'. The closer the English smugglers were to the Continent the rougher became not only the names of their groups but also their methods of operating. Certainly in Kent and Sussex the Farnham Blacks, the Mayfield Gang, Ruxley's Crew, the Groombridge Gang and, most notorious of all, the dreaded Hawkhurst Gang were far more vicious than the 'Whitewigs' of Isaac Gulliver, the famous king of the Dorsetshire smugglers, or the celebrated Carter family of Prussia Cove down on Mount's Bay far to the west in Cornwall.

Proximity to the Continent and the entrepôts from which they bought their contraband made the smugglers of Kent, Sussex and East Anglia complacent in their commerce, and contemptuous of all efforts on the part of the forces of law and order to stop them carrying it on. There was, however, another factor which contributed to this feeling of superiority in the contrabandists of the south-east corner of Britain: these smugglers had the largest market in the land almost on their doorstep – the capital city, London, with its numberless criminal confraternity containing the smugglers' accomplices and agents. It is little wonder, then, that these south-eastern smugglers were so sure of themselves, so bold in their opposition to the Revenue officers and even to the king's soldiers and sailors who were sent against them when their outrages became too much for the authorities to brook.

At the other end of England's southern coast the smugglers were the hardiest of all, for their county, Cornwall, was surrounded by sea, battered by the Atlantic Ocean, indented with coves and protected by fearsome rocks and shoals. Cornishmen were both merchants and smugglers, as well as wreckers, privateers and even pirates.

The best-known smuggling name in Cornwall is undoubtedly that of

Carter: not a gang nor a company, but a family. The coves of Mount's Bay had been favourite landing-places for smugglers for many years, and the Carters favoured above all of them Prussia Cove, which they used for their illicit and highly successful trade for over forty years. John Carter was the head of the family and humorously called himself 'The King of Prussia'. Harry was his second-in-command and ensured posthumous fame for himself when he published his autobiography in 1809. John was actually born in 1738, the eldest-but-one of the seven Carter brothers, who grew to young manhood as rather poor fisherfolk. Only John and the youngest brother received any schooling: Harry educated himself at a later stage, no doubt helped by his brothers, and specialized in mathematics, his arithmetical studies standing him in good stead when the family business of full-time smuggling started up and he could officiate as accountant, one of the most efficient 'quill-drivers' in the history of English smuggling. Before he reached this position he tried mining, and then joined his brothers in their fishing business, from which it was but a short step to smuggling.

John was making enough money for himself and his family by 1770 to build a fine family house at Prussia (or King's) Cove. Appropriately, he named the new house 'The King's House'; beneath it, sure enough, was a king's warehouse, as the Customs house cellars were always named, in the form of a huge natural cavern, so typical of Cornish coves, which John improved and fitted out as an extensive contraband store. Under John's direction, the Carters built a neat little harbour for themselves and cut a road up the cliffs for the better transportation of their merchandise. Such provision of facilities by a smuggling organization is unique in the history of the craft, and not only shows the Carters' determination, forethought, ingenuity and assurance, but also the complete ineffectuality of the local Customs forces to do anything to prevent their astonishing smuggling activities. Perhaps only Cornishmen could have carried out their designs with such *élan*. These were topped off by the final piece of impudence: a platform was built on which was mounted a battery of eight six-pounder cannon for the defence of Prussia Cove.

With fishing put aside, the Carters, under John's firm direction, built up a large clientele among the local gentry and the substantial burgesses of the few towns of which Cornwall could boast. The Carters became known for their pin-point punctuality in the delivery of their contraband to their customers; and as for determination, the family from Prussia Cove had a smack of the dreaded Hawkhurst Gang of Kent when they raided the Poole Customs House, for when the king's men seized a cargo going into the cove and took it to Penzance for safe-keeping, John immediately called up an armed posse, rode to Penzance and broke open the king's warehouse. He made sure his men took only those commodities which he knew to be his, and returned unmolested to Prussia Cove.

While John tended to oversee the family on land, Harry made his name as a smuggling captain at sea. By the time he was twenty-five he had his own ship; and soon he had an even better vessel: a 50 ton cutter with a crew of ten prime smugglers. He allowed no swearing on board and enforced a strict discipline, which contributed to the continuously successful string of smuggling ventures. When the American War of Independence broke out the Carter brothers easily obtained Letters of Marque for five of their ships, which in this way became privateers, entitled to capture enemy vessels and immune to impressment into the Royal Navy. Little is known of just how the Carters used these ships and the special privileges they enjoyed, but their fortune continued to increase and not merely from smuggling.

The collector of Poole had called the famous Dorset smuggler Isaac Gulliver 'a man of great speculating genius', and in his autobiography Harry Carter described his kin as 'a speculating family'. It was this genius for speculation which marked out the really successful smuggler from the also-rans and the occasionally profit-making free trader. The art was in being prepared to switch from one commodity to another as the duties altered so that the greatest profit could be made. However, that was not the whole story: the makers of fortunes were those who kept the contraband coming across the Channel so that it was a real traffic: constant, steady and of huge volume. It was of little use waking up one day and deciding to take the ship over to France, bringing the contraband back, selling it and then living off the proceeds until necessity again prompted replenishment of one's purse. Full-scale and constant trade was the only way to ensure success in smuggling just as it was in legitimate commerce.

The Carters' good fortune could not last, and it was Harry who fell first upon evil days. One day while out sailing the Channel in his splendid cutter something broke on board and he had to put into St Malo for repairs. The French port authorities did not like the look of the ship's papers and they decided Harry was safer in gaol, for they suspected he was, in fact, a pirate who had been preying on French ships. He could hardly blame them: he was a registered privateer, as his papers must have shown, and the line between pirate and privateer was fine at the best of times. The affair gives some indication of what the Carters did in the five ships granted Letters of Marque when they were not smuggling. John arrived in St Malo hoping to secure the release of his brother, but the French authorities promptly arrested him as well and also put him in gaol. Amazingly enough, the lords of the Admiralty were asked to help the two smuggling Cornish brothers and they used their good offices to secure the captains' release from their prison in St Malo. The French authorities only agreed to this when the Admiralty agreed to release two French officers in exchange. This incident again indicates how important the Carters were to their country, and one can only speculate what services they were carrying out at sea for the British government to secure their release from foreign imprisonment. When one remembers how they carried on their smuggling trade in Prussia Cove, making thousands of pounds every year while the local Customs forces did nothing to close down their operations, for many years, the only possible conclusion can be that they enjoyed an immunity paralleled only, once again, by Isaac Gulliver.

The French authorities had released Harry and John but they kept Harry's cutter, and when the two brothers eventually reached home they suffered another blow on discovering that their stay-at-home siblings had been letting the business slide into debt. They soon put things right, and, after an initial setback, when he was again mistaken for a pirate, Harry, thanks once more to the intervention of the lords of the Admiralty, was soon back in his successful smuggling stride.

All went well with the Carters' business and their remarkable base in Prussia Cove until the year 1788. One day Harry was running a cargo at Cawsand, a favourite smugglers' beach on the west side of Plymouth Sound, from his cutter the *Revenge*, when two rowing-boats appeared just as he was opening his hatches. He was in a trap, in fact, for the Revenue cutter *Busy* had been watching him and had called up HMS *Druid*, a Royal Navy frigate. Harry and his smugglers watched horrified as the boats came on, and their crews swarmed aboard and set about them. In the ferocious fight which followed a seaman was killed and several were severely wounded. Harry Carter himself was badly wounded in the head and fell to his own deck where he was left for dead as the fight carried on. He came to and, unnoticed, silently slipped over the side and swam ashore into the arms of the landing-party, which was being directed by his brother Charles as the lander. Charles managed to get his fearfully wounded brother to his house, where he was treated by their doctor. It was here that they learned that Harry now had a price on his head: £300, which would be paid by the authorities for information leading to his arrest for murder.

Harry was taken on to a safer house, the residence of a local gentleman who was a loyal customer. Then he was moved again, this time to Acton Castle, where the doctor came to attend to him once more, after being blindfolded so that he could not give away the location if questioned by the king's men. It was not until three months had passed that Harry was fit enough to make his way, by night, back home to the family stronghold in Prussia Cove. By this time the £300 offer had expired. Not surprisingly, Harry had had enough of smuggling, at least for the time being, and when his wife was diagnosed as having terminal tuberculosis a few weeks later, he decided it was time to leave the country, and so set sail for America. There he embraced Methodism, took up farming on Long Island and eventually decided to return home in 1790. Rather misguidedly, he started preaching his new-found faith in public before anyone could stop him, but his family persuaded him it was an unwise career move and managed to spirit him overseas again, for the authorities were still looking for him. This time he went to Roscoff, the great smugglers' entrepôt in Britanny. Here he was made welcome by the smugglers' merchants and the other English fugitives from justice; it was not long before he was at his preaching again, conducting regular Sunday afternoon services on the great stone pier of the busy port. His congregation comprised the English expatriates of Roscoff, as well as the captains and crews of ships, usually smugglers, from such smuggling centres as the Channel Islands. Harry must have felt even more at home when he met the men from the privateering ships which used the port as their base, even though he himself had given up such a dangerous occupation.

War between Britain and France broke out in 1793 and Harry's agreeable life in Roscoff came to an abrupt end: all Englishmen in the town were immediately placed under house arrest. When he was released in 1795, it was home to Prussia Cove that he went as fast as he could. However, Harry did not return to the free trade, he chose instead to continue the agricultural activities he had tried in the New World. He took a smallholding not far from Prussia Cove, and found that it was safe to pursue his vocation as a Methodist lay-preacher once again. He died in 1829 at the ripe old age of eighty, and still in debt.

The year before Harry returned, the authorities had at last summoned up enough courage to do something about the nest of notorious smugglers and privateers in Prussia Cove. It may well have been a token gesture, perhaps some new Customs officer had been outraged at what he discovered about the Carters, but no one knows why the Collector of Customs at Penzance suddenly decided to attack. He had persuaded the commanding officer of the Helston and Penzance Volunteers, whose main purpose was to guard Mount's Bay against invasion by the French, to assist him. So a rather half-hearted attack was mounted, the Volunteers going into the cove and opening fire on the battery of guns and the men manning them. The Volunteers then charged with a will and carried the position, the six-pounders useless in such close-quarter fighting, rounded up the smugglers and began the process of dismantling the eight-gun battery.

While all this was going on, the people of the neighbouring clifftops rushed to Prussia Cove and delivered their attack on the Volunteers with sticks, stones and even a few firearms. One shot caught an officer in the head, and the Volunteers fired into the mob of enraged Carter supporters, who decided to withdraw.

Of the Carters themselves there was no sign, and the forces of law and order returned to the Penzance Customs House with little more than wounded pride and thirteen barrels of assorted spirits. The next step was the issue of warrants for the arrest of every Carter brother; however, in the event, the authorities were unable to find any constable willing to enter Prussia Cove without a large military escort. The commanding officer of the Helston Garrison was requested to assist in this matter by the Customs officers, but he would not go into the Carter stronghold without having received a direct order from the War Office in London.

The smuggling brothers simply repaired their defences, replenished their contraband stock and went on free trading. Will Richards, John's son-in-law, took over command, and John himself died in 1803. The King of Prussia was dead, but it wasn't a case of 'Long live the king'. Will Richards could not manage to keep the business going, and soon the lease on Prussia Cove was advertised for sale, the bills enumerating '. . . all those large and commodious cellars, lofts, salt-houses, fish-presses, boat-beds, capstans, . . . together with the said Cove and landing-places therein. The above premises are exceedingly well adapted and situated for carrying on any kind of trade.' But no one was keen to emulate the Carters, and they continued smuggling until a preventive boat was stationed in Prussia Cove as part of the coastal blockade. Then, when the Coast Guard was formed, a station was built in 1825; not even the Carters could carry on in Prussia Cove after that.[1]

Isaac Gulliver was born in 1745 in the village of Semington in Wiltshire. His father was a smuggler, and by the age of twelve the boy was working alongside him at the trade which was flourishing along the coast of the county of Dorset. Isaac grew tall, with a commanding presence, and an air of quiet authority which made men happy to serve him. He bought his first property – an inn with strong smuggling connections near Blandford Forum in Dorset – and he must have enjoyed success in his free trading for other properties followed in regular succession. Several of them were on known smuggling routes, most of them up from the great smuggling beaches between Poole and Hengistbury Head, where the genteel resort of Bournemouth now stands. The famous 'chines', or narrow valleys cut through the cliffs by streams, made ideal roadways for the swift transport of contraband off the beaches, in the stage of running when the smugglers were most vulnerable. At the height of his trading, Gulliver had a fleet of fifteen luggers working for him, neither privateering nor fishing: just running contraband goods. His trains of tubmen, packhorses and farm-waggons stretched for miles, and often he was seen directing them mounted on a great white horse, the epitome of the romantic smuggling chief, but very real nevertheless.

It was at Kinson that Gulliver built his own residence, a strategically placed village in the north of present-day Bournemouth, from where he and his lieutenants could watch and direct the vast smuggling operations

West Howe Lodge, Kinson, near Bournemouth in Dorset, the purpose-
built stronghold of Isaac Gulliver

which were now his *modus operandi*. Here Gulliver built his ideal house,
fit for a king of smugglers, with crenellations outside, thick walls
between, and secret rooms inside, such as the largest which had its
entrance half-way up the main chimney, and the vast cellar which was
entered through a trap door in the dining-room floor, always covered by
the carpet. From this unique house led several tunnels, one going
southwards towards the sea and a good 6 ft high. Gulliver lived in this
house, West Howe Lodge, between 1780 and 1816, as and when his
business trips allowed, and when he was not in residence he had plenty
of other dwellings to choose from in the county. One was Gulliver's
Farm and is still called that on the Ordnance Survey map today.

By 1776, when he was aged thirty-one, Isaac Gulliver had a network
of houses and farms in which storehouses had been constructed for the
receiving and distribution of the vast amounts of contraband that he was
handling at this stage of his career. As well as the fleet of fifteen ships
which brought the uncustomed goods on to the Dorsetshire shores, he
had a company of fifty smugglers whom he decked out in his own
uniform: a stout canvas smock of the sort worn for centuries by Dorset

Halt: smugglers by Henry Perlee Parker, portraying Isaac Gulliver and his men

shepherds, hard-wearing and eminently practical for the rough work necessary, and a long-haired wig dressed with wig-powder and tied off the face in a neat, seaman-like pony-tail. Wig-powder was one of the most popular commodities Gulliver smuggled, and so it was fitting that those who actually brought it into the country should make good use of it. They were known up and down the country as 'Gulliver's White Wigs'.

This picture, entitled *Halt: smugglers*, was painted by Henry Perlee Parker, and there is considerable evidence to support the claim that it actually portrays Gulliver and his men resting after a stiff pull up from some Dorset beach. Gulliver, an almost Garibaldi-like figure with his shirt, braces and steel-soled boots, is happily chatting with his men, and all around are interesting smuggling details: the men are refreshing themselves with some of the goods they are smuggling, brandy, gin, sliced meat and even what looks like Bath Olivers. Behind them rest two of the packhorses so widely used along the Dorset and Hampshire coasts, of which there was such a plentiful supply in the New Forest with its famous ponies.

By 1778 Gulliver had land as far as the western border of the county where he bought North Eggardon farm, which still snuggles under the great Iron Age hill fortress of Eggardon Hill. Five miles from the sea, this lofty height was used by Gulliver's smuggling captains as a seamark when they were coming in with their contraband cargoes, using a lamp to mark it by night and a grove of trees specially planted by Gulliver for the purpose by day. Today the trees have gone, cut down by jealous Customs men, but it is possible to see exactly where they stood, for the octagonal bank which protected them is still there. The goods which his men landed below Eggardon went along what is today known as Gulliver's Lane, through the country ways and on to such huge markets as the cities of Bath and Bristol.

Gulliver was known as 'the gentle smuggler', for it was his claim that he had never had to harm a king's officer in the pursuance of his business, but there seems to have been more to it than this. When asked for a report on Gulliver's activities, the Collector of Customs for the port of Poole told his masters on the Board of Customs in London: 'He is a person of great speculating genius, and besides this he has carried on a variety of other businesses, but we find that he is not known at present to be concerned in any sort of merchandise, and lives retired at a farm in the neighbourhood, having acquired, as it is reported, a very considerable property.' By 1791 he was being described as 'a Dorset merchant', and he always signed himself: Isaac Gulliver '. . . of Kinson, Wine Merchant'. The probability is that Gulliver enjoyed immunity from prosecution. Legend has it that one of his smuggling ships spotted a French squadron making for the Dorset coast at Weymouth where King George III was on holiday, the enemy's intention being nothing short of a royal assassination. The smuggling captain was able to tell the nearest Royal Naval squadron, which made for the French and chased them off, foiling their murderous attempt against the British king. The story was told to George III, who immediately cried in gratitude: 'Let Gulliver smuggle as he will, then!'

And smuggle he did: even after 1782. That was the year in which the government offered a free pardon to any smuggler who would give up his illegal ways and enter the Royal Navy; alternatively, the smuggler could find a substitute to enter the service on his behalf. There was much surprise in Dorset when Gulliver announced he was applying for the free pardon and providing a substitute. He also said that he would be moving to Devon where he would do nothing but sell fine wines and spirits to the local gentry.

Gulliver was now seen more often riding the countryside of Devon apparently taking orders from his well-heeled customers, but he was no doubt buying more property and setting out more storerooms and safe routes for his smugglers. The commissioners of Customs in London were not deceived, for in 1788 they asked the Poole collector for a report on Gulliver's smuggling activities, if any. The collector told London that although Gulliver had been one of the most successful smugglers in the West Country, he had changed his ways after accepting the free pardon and was now a legitimate wine merchant, opening vaults in remote places, and selling his wares duty paid but at prices well below those of his competitors. It is difficult to believe that anyone was taken in by this.

In 1800 Isaac Gulliver made his last smuggling run. This was reported in *The Gentlemen's Magazine*, which described the smuggling caravan 'at the head of which rode the Old Chief, mounted on a spirited charger'. Gulliver was a popular figure to both common and gentlefolk alike in Dorset, for everyone was indebted to him in some way or other.

By the time he really did retire Isaac Gulliver was a millionaire: he moved back to West Howe Lodge, Kinson, in 1815, and two years after that he made his last move to the Dorset town of Wimborne Minster, where his large house stands, still named Gulliver House. *The Gentlemen's Magazine* now described him as 'Mr. Gulliver, who was formerly a smuggler of disreputable notoriety', for he was now a warden of the great Minster church. Gulliver became one of the sights of Wimborne, wheeled round the streets in his bath-chair by his dutiful daughter, whom he married well into one of the great banking families of the county. He made a will which ran into many pages and was twelve thousand words in length, in which he distributed to his heirs properties in Dorset, Hampshire, Wiltshire and Somerset, as well as large amounts of money in bequests. The will also directed that his daughter's male descendants, for his only son and heir Isaac had died at the untimely age of twenty-three, 'who derived benefit from his will, should apply for, and endeavour to obtain, an Act of Parliament, or proper Licence from the Crown, to enable him to take, use and bear the Surname and Arms of Gulliver'.

Gulliver died on 13 September 1822, a fact which was reported in newspapers throughout the land, and he was buried with great pomp and dignity in the Minster church. His tombstone was inscribed with the simple words: 'Isaac Gulliver, Esquire'.[2]

The counties of Sussex and Kent were, without doubt, the most troublesome to the forces of law and order in the war against smuggling, their proximity not only to the continent of Europe, but also to the greatest market for contraband, London, being the main cause. Of all the contraband smuggled into the country, a full quarter came into Kent and Sussex. Here, the free traders were far more determined and ruthless than their counterparts further west along the coast, and they had a far longer tradition of smuggling: it was in these counties, particularly in the area known as the Romney Marshes, that wool had been smuggled <u>out</u> of the country as long ago as the reign of King Edward I of England. Their viciousness and contempt for the king's writ was deeply ingrained very early in their unsavoury history, and they felt little patriotism: it was from the county of Kent that cannons, cast in the foundries of the great Kentish ironmasters of the Weald, were smuggled out of the country to King Philip II of Spain for use by his ships against England in the Great Armada of 1588 and later years.

In Kent and Sussex the smugglers did not use the word 'company' for their association, but rather the far more sinister word 'gang'; they lived up to it too, behaving very much like the gangsters of a later and equally barbarous period. The leaders of these gangs were not running family businesses, nor were they skilful merchants who chose to trade freely rather than within the law, but men of violence, more like the warlords of medieval times on their own fiefs and manors, maintaining reigns of terror and conducting armed insurrection against the forces of the lawful government whenever it suited them. They were for the most part, to put it frankly, vicious outlaws.

As early as 1724 Daniel Defoe, in *A Tour Thro' the Whole Island of Great Britain*, wrote of his journey through Romney Marsh:

As I rode along this coast, I perceived several dragoons, Riding Officers and others armed and on horse-back, riding always as if they were huntsmen beating up their game. Upon inquiry I found their diligence was in quest of owlers, as they call them, and sometimes they catch some of them; but when I came to enquire further I found too often that oftentimes they are attacked in the night with such numbers that they dare not resist them, or, if they do, as it were, to stand still and see the wool carried off before their faces, not daring to meddle.

And of the south coast of England generally Defoe wrote that he did not 'find any foreign commerce except it be what we call smuggling and roguing, which, I may say, is the reigning commerce of all this part of the English coast, from the mouth of the Thames to Land's End of Cornwall.' It was to get much worse.

Defoe only saw the smuggling out of wool; six years later tea and spirits were being run into these counties as a far more profitable traffic. And by 1740 the smuggling in Kent and Sussex had really taken off: no less a personage than Admiral Vernon, that same 'Old Grog' who introduced the mixture of pure spirits and water into the Royal Navy, wrote in a letter to His Lordships of the Admiralty in 1745:

I can't but think it is a seasonable time to suggest to Your Lordships that there are said to be in the town of Deal no less than two hundred able young men and sea-faring people who are known to have no visible way of getting a living but by the infamous trade of smuggling, many keeping a horse and arms to be ready at all calls.

At Dover it is conjectured that there may be found four hundred at a time ready to smuggle, at Ramsgate and Folkestone three hundred each; and it is said that within these three weeks no less than nine cutters at a time have gone off from Folkestone to Boulogne; and that it is conjectured that from the town of Folkestone itself a thousand pounds a week is run over to Boulogne in the smuggling way; and about six or seven days past a Dover cutter landed goods in the night under the castle that was carried off by a party of sixty horses, and the cutter supposed to have done it came into Dover pier next day; and although most believed it was she, no one proceeded against them to make inquiry about it. This smuggling has converted those employed in it, first from honest, industrious fishermen to lazy, drunken profligate smugglers, and now to dangerous spies on all our proceedings, for the enemy's [France's] daily information.

As this passes within my observation, I should think it criminal in me not to inform you of it; I can't but think it a national reproach upon us to have let their villainy and treachery run to such extensive lengths.[3]

Fifty years later the situation was much worse in every aspect: Old Grog was something of a prophet, but even he did not believe that successive governments would be unable to cope with the inexorable rise of the threat which smuggling posed to the well-being of the country. If only the authorities could have concentrated their efforts on the cradle of English smuggling: the county of Kent, and Romney Marsh as its epicentre. However, they did not and the gangs grew and prospered, spreading their malign influence all over the garden of England and far beyond.

Of all the smuggling gangs the Hawkhurst Gang was without doubt the very worst. It was led in its heyday by two of the vilest villains smuggling or any other illegal occupation ever produced: Thomas Kingsmill and Arthur Gray. Their HQ was the little village of Hawkhurst just north of Hastings, but they operated with their gang from that notorious smuggling town Deal right the way along the coasts of Sussex, Hampshire, Dorset and Devon.

Every man in the gang was extremely proud to be a member. By 1749 the Hawkhurst Gang was firmly under the control of the Gray brothers, Arthur and William, both already rich on the proceeds of smuggling. Arthur had built himself a fine big house, with its own secret storehouse, at Seacox Heath near Hawkhurst. The gang's favourite base was the famous Mermaid Inn at Rye, where they provided a local sight as they sat planning their ventures, their weapons to hand, ready for any emergency.

When they were drunk they would swagger about, frightening people and firing off their guns just for the sheer pleasure of seeing sober citizens jump. No one ever refused to lend his farm-waggon to them or enquired too closely into their affairs, for their hold over the area was complete.

The Hawkhurst outfit was not the only gang in Kent, far from it, but unlike the bootlegging gangs in American cities they did not fight each other for territory and would even help each other when really big runs and jobs were in the offing. However, things could go wrong, for the

Hawkhurst Gang was very touchy about what it considered to belong to it by rights: on one occasion the Hawkhurst men had asked the help of the Wingham crew to carry inland a huge cargo of tea, which had been run into Sandwich Bay. The Wingham men made the mistake of carrying off what they considered to be their share of the teabags before the full load was ashore. On seeing what was happening, the Hawkhurst men chased after their luckless partners, hacked many of them to pieces with the cutlasses which were their favourite weapons, and grabbed back the tea and the horses carrying them.

But it was not only fellow-smugglers that the Hawkhurst men attacked: in 1744 they had set upon the riding officers of Shoreham as they were landing a cargo, for the king's men had dared to challenge them. They severely wounded the officers, seized their horses and weapons, and then marched them off like prisoners-of-war to the gang's headquarters in Hawkhurst. Here they interrogated their prisoners and discovered that two of them had actually been members of the gang long before (another case of poachers turned game-keepers), and this made them very angry. They dragged the two officers off to a nearby wood, tied them to trees and, Navy-style, flogged them to within an inch of their lives. The gang then sent them across the Channel in one of their own ships and had them turned loose on what was, in that year, enemy soil, still dressed in their king's uniforms.

The worms, however, were about to turn: by 1747 the local people of the Weald, where the Hawkhurst Gang's reign of terror was felt most, had had enough. They had seen that there was no help to be expected from the forces of the Crown: the outrage committed upon the riding officers of Shoreham had shown them that, and even those men had got off lightly compared with many of the gang's other victims. It was in the village of Goudhurst that the spark of resistance was first struck. Less than 6 miles from the gang's HQ in Hawkhurst, the village worthies decided that their only course of action was to form themselves into a vigilante force to be known as the Goudhurst Militia. Command was given to John Sturt, a young man who had been a sergeant in a foot regiment of the line, and soon 'General' Sturt was training every able-bodied villager who had put his hand to a written declaration of their intentions. This news soon got to Hawkhurst, and Thomas Kingsmill, a native of Goudhurst, was thrown into a fury. He immediately led the gang against Goudhurst, attacking the defences that had been thrown up and driving the militia back inside them. Then Kingsmill sent in a snatch-squad which collared one of the defenders and took him off to Hawkhurst for interrogation under torture. All of Sturt's dispositions were revealed, and the mangled man was sent back to his village with the message that the gang would attack at noon on 20 April 1747, and put to the sword every man, woman and child, afterwards burning the village to the ground.

Sturt set his people to a furious fortifying of the village, with trenches and strong-points, and the women and children were sent away for safety. The church and its churchyard were prepared as the village's redoubt, the final bastion of their desperate defence. Sure enough, the

Goudhurst church, Kent, the citadel of the Goudhurst militia

smugglers appeared on time and surrounded the village; Kingsmill formally called on Sturt to surrender, in correct military procedure, and on receiving the defenders' refusal, ordered his ruffians to open fire. The volley returned by the militia was more than the smugglers had bargained for, and several smugglers fell, including Kingsmill's brother George, who died beside him. The fire-fight which ensued showed how well Sturt had done his job and the gang had to beat a retreat, with most of their number wounded and two dead. With a loud huzza the Goudhurst men issued from their defences and chased the smugglers back to Hawkhurst.

It was not, of course, the end of the Hawkhurst Gang for by the September of the same year it was as strong as ever and even more bloody-minded than before. Such an organization, which lasted for decades, had the characteristic of the snake of ancient belief: it could reassemble its parts after they had been severed and be whole again, and many times more venomous. The government had actually done something in the months since the showdown at Goudhurst: it had cut the duty on tea, and the south coast smugglers were very edgy about their future fiscal prospects, for tea had been their staple stock-in-trade. It was in this mood that the Hawkhurst Gang awaited the landing of a huge cargo of tea that September, being brought in by a cutter named *The Three Brothers* of Guernsey. However, out at sea this cutter was caught by another: the *Swift*, the Poole Revenue vessel, commanded by Captain William Johnson. He had received a tip-off about the planned run, no doubt communicated to him by yet another enemy of the Hawkhurst Gang. *The Three Brothers* was seized by the Revenuers and a prize crew put aboard, and she was taken into the nearest port, which happened to be Poole in Dorset. The cargo of tea and some accompanying kegs of spirits were lodged in the king's warehouse in Poole, which was located, of course, in the vast cellars of the Customs House on the famous Poole Quay.

Several of the crew of *The Three Brothers* had got away from their pursuers in the ship's cockboat, and they eventually reached Hawkhurst and broke the bad news to the gang. Thomas Kingsmill, then in command, became angry as he realized that after the Goudhurst débâcle the Hawkhurst Gang would be a laughing-stock on both sides of the trenches in the smuggling war, once it got out that they had had a cargo seized by the Revenue men. Kingsmill immediately detailed sixty of his strongest and most aggressive men to draw as many weapons as they could carry from the gang's extensive armoury. Swords, pistols, cutlasses, carbines, blunderbusses, muskets, axes, pick-axes, jemmies and crow-bars were taken, so that they would be ready for every eventuality on their recovery expedition. Kingsmill then briefed his ruffians, telling them what had happened to *their* tea, and that they were off to Poole to get it back. They set out all mounted, going across Sussex into Hampshire, where they made use of the services of a group of free traders who had also not been doing very well of late, these men having to sign a bond which the gang produced and which ensured their assistance come what might. Here was yet another example of the formality with which this dreadful outfit conducted their affairs when it suited them, putting them almost on a par with the official groups of king's officers against whom they constantly found themselves opposed.

On they went into the New Forest, for all the world like a squadron of the king's dragoons, until they reached its capital, Lyndhurst, where they put up for the night, with no one asking who they were. The next day they continued on their way, unchallenged by any magistrate or other king's officer. Through Minstead they rode, dining at Fritham with the landlord of the Royal Oak, who was a great friend of all smugglers. Then on through Fordingbridge, the western gateway of the New Forest, where they were warmly greeted by many of the townsfolk who knew very well who they were. They reached the port of Poole in Dorset at last and halted on the top of Constitution Hill to survey their target: the Customs house on the quay, which they had come to raid. As darkness fell the force commander sent two of his men as scouts to reconnoitre the target-area. They returned with the unwelcome intelligence that the Customs house had one of His Majesty's sloops-of-war moored to the quay alongside it. The ship's guns were covering the doors of the warehouse by which the gang intended to make their entry. On hearing this many of the smugglers voted to go back east; but the second scout spoke up and assured Kingsmill that the tide was on the ebb and the ship would soon be too far below the top of the quay to be any danger to them. Kingsmill agreed and ordered the raiding-party to go down into the town. They met no one as they silently threaded their way through the narrow streets and soon they were on the quay. They

The Hawkhurst Gang raiding the Custom House at Poole, Dorset, in 1747

quickly had the doors of the Customs house cellars open, and shortly thereafter they found their tea and the brandy-kegs which accompanied it. There were plenty of other seized goods in the warehouse, but the Hawkhurst men took only what was theirs. They were neither greedy nor larcenous, or so they believed, and wanted only what they thought had been wrongfully taken from them by the Customs men. They loaded the goods onto the pack-horses and were soon making their way out of the town. Still no one challenged them, nor, as far as they knew, even saw them, or so it appeared.

They reached Fordingbridge just as dawn was breaking and breakfasted at the George Inn. They then borrowed two steelyards, weighed the tea and shared it out among themselves. Then they set off once more and as they passed out of the little town they were cheered by the early-morning crowd which had gathered to see them in their triumphal progress, for by now the Fordingbridgians had learned what the Hawkhurst Gang had accomplished. Without any challenge by authority, the Hawkhurst Gang eventually reached home. It was by no means the only assault on a Customs house, but it was certainly the most audacious, the best planned and the least challenged.

The challenge came later: naturally there were informers who wished to damage the gang irreparably, for a large reward was offered by the Board of Customs in London. A man who turned king's evidence had been tossed a bag of tea by one of the smugglers named Diamond as the cavalcade had ridden in triumph out of Fordingbridge; but this had not been enough to remind him of the terrible vengeance which the Hawkhurst Gang would exact upon him when they found out what he had done. It so happened that Diamond had already been arrested on suspicion of involvement in the raid on the Poole Customs House. The collector at Southampton sent one of his men, an elderly tide-waiter named Galley, to escort the informer, Chater, to Sussex and the home of the magistrate who was due to hear the case against Diamond. But as they journeyed through Sussex they were taken prisoner by local smugglers who had found out about their mission, set them on one horse tied together, and led them back towards Hawkhurst, there to be kept as prisoners until the hue and cry over the Poole raid was over. That was the intention of the smugglers, but some of their womenfolk intervened and said that as Chater and Galley were about to get the Hawkhurst boys hanged, the smugglers should string up the two prisoners and so get in first with yet another snook cocked at authority. However, the men contented themselves with torturing and whipping the unfortunates as they led them ever closer to Hawkhurst. Eventually Galley, terribly mutilated, fell off the horse he had been set on, more dead than alive. The smugglers decided to anticipate his end a little and buried him in a shallow, sandy grave while he was still breathing.

The smuggler-torturers were in a quandary over the informer Chater, because they wanted to make his end so horrible that it would deter informers for a long time to come. They kept him locked up for two days while they argued. Then they took him out, cut him about savagely with a knife and then tried to hang him from the windlass of a well, but the rope was too short. They slashed the rope and the wretched man fell down the shaft, where he lay terribly injured as his tormentors dropped stones on him until the shaft was full and he was finally put out of his misery.

The law took six months to catch up with them, and that only happened when one of the murderers was flung into gaol on an entirely different charge and decided to turn king's evidence. This resulted in a royal proclamation listing the murderers' names and demanding their surrender on pain of being declared outlaws. £500 was offered as a reward for information leading to the arrest of any of the smugglers involved. Soon seven murderers were in custody, and, at a special assize at Chichester, all were convicted and sent for execution. Soon after, Kingsmill was arrested with four of his gang-members: they were tried at the Old Bailey itself in London on the charge of breaking into His Majesty's Customs house and warehouse in Poole. The prosecution described the crime as 'the most unheard-of act of villainy and impudence ever known'. Kingsmill and his lieutenant, Fairall, were condemned to death, but to the end they proclaimed that they were innocent because the tea and spirits had been their own property, bought and paid for! They remained defiant right up to the point of their deaths; afterwards their corpses were exhibited on gibbets in their respective villages as the grimmest warning possible to other like-minded smugglers.

The Hawkhurst crew was by no means the only vicious smuggling gang in Kent and Sussex. The Groombridge Gang, for example, were operating on Romney Marsh as early as 1733. One of their convoys was heading inland when it was chased by riding officers at Stonecrouch. The smugglers halted, turned and grabbed the officers, disarming them and taking them as prisoners to their HQ in the village of Groombridge. They were, however, released after their weapons had been smashed and handed back to them. It was this sort of insolent trick that distinguished such gangs in their dealings with anyone foolish enough to tangle with them. The village of Groombridge was strategically placed on the smugglers' principal route to their main market, London. Its smugglers habitually went down to the coast at Fairlight, Lydd and Pevensey, took the goods that had been run in there and shipped them back up to London. The gang was not averse to working with the Hawkhurst men, as well as with other outfits such as the Hooe Company, and they were just as tyrannical as the most infamous of these organizations. So contemptuous of authority were the members of such gangs that there is record of several of them returning from the colonies after being transported there for their smuggling crimes. Others were perfectly capable of escaping even when troops of soldiers were sent to capture them.

However, the gang which bade fair to outdo the Hawkhurst mob in wickedness was Ruxley's Crew. It hailed from Hastings and had more in common with pirates than with smugglers, for in 1768 members of the gang boarded a Dutch ship in the Downs for the apparent purpose of making a bid for the contraband *The Three Sisters* was carrying. Suddenly a row broke out while the smuggler-pirates were negotiating with the captain: the latter was cut down and killed, and most of the crew put to the sword, a chopping stroke to the spine being used. The Ruxley Crew returned to their home port boasting about what they had done; it was not long before the story got back to London and a regiment of the Inniskilling Dragoons, later known throughout the Army as 'The Skins', was dispatched to arrest the murderers. It took a complete day of fighting before they could be arrested, and as a witness at their subsequent trial said: 'Of all the monstrous wickedness with which this age abounds, nothing, I will be bound to say, can parallel the senses of villainy that were laid bare . . . the judges themselves declared that in all their reading they never met with such a combined sense of barbarity, so deliberately carried on and so cruelly executed!' The criminals of the Ruxley Crew had had to be taken to London after their arrest in a man-o'-war, escorted by a cutter, so great was the danger of their being rescued by the members of some of the other vicious gangs along that coast. And it was from the date of this incident that all Hastings seamen, whether fishermen, smugglers, or both, were known nationwide as 'Chopbacks', because of the way the Ruxley Crew had hacked the backbones of the wretched Dutchmen.[4]

The ordinary, nameless smugglers must not be forgotten: the tub-carriers, the pony-leaders, the batmen, the wagonners, and the swimming smugglers, who, under water, guided the great rafts of sunken kegs to the shore. For every Carter, Rattenbury, Kingsmill and Gulliver there were thousands of unknowns who faced hard labour, danger and death to get the goods along the smuggling routes.

The tubman, known in some areas as a flasker, was paid 5d. a night just for turning up at the spot arranged by the lander; and he got 25d. if the run was successful, which it usually was. So, for a man who worked from dawn to dusk in the farmer's fields for a shilling a week (if the farmer was feeling generous and the price of corn was high), smugglers' pay was pretty good. Often there were perks: some tea, perhaps a little brandy, and maybe even a hot meal into the bargain. Certainly, very successful smugglers like Isaac Gulliver could afford to treat their men well: in the painting of Gulliver and his men resting from their labours, by Henry Perlee ('Smuggler') Parker, they are enjoying a picnic with plenty of food and drink, much of it from the contraband they are running. The contented state of these smugglers is apparent.

Of course, it must be remembered that regular farm labourers could be laid off without warning and with no compensation nor parish relief. And whenever farmers could cut their workers' wages they did: the famous Tolpuddle Martyrs of Dorset were charged not with demanding higher wages but with forming an association or union to maintain the level of their wages. The quickest way to deal with a man complaining about his wages was to give him the sack on the spot, the very term 'sack' having obvious agricultural associations. A labourer so dealt with might well have turned immediately to the free trade, where he knew he could make a week's slave-wages in one night. Smuggling may have been hard, illegal and dangerous, but it was so profitable that the risks were worthwhile; and having received churlish treatment at the hands of the farmer, who was an authority and establishment figure, the turning to outlawry was a revenge which must have been sweet to the man who had lost all.

Thomas Hardy's house at Higher Bockhampton near Dorchester was on a main smuggling route up from the coast, and its outbuildings were regularly used as a contraband dump in the first quarter of the last century. A family servant had been a tubman and it was from him that the young Hardy learned how harsh the carrying of kegs had been. This old man was broken-winded and his chest had actually suffered permanent damage by carrying pairs of barrels over many miles by night, as well as in the daytime too. Each barrel, custom-built in the special manufactories in the Channel Islands, was linked to another by tarred ropes which were tied to wire hoops at each end, so that a harness was formed, and held just under 4½ gallons. To appreciate that sort of burden we must imagine the weight of each barrel on chest and back, the ropes cutting into the tubman's shoulders and jarring painfully with every step as he tottered along rough paths, up hill and down, through woods and gorse-screens, mostly in the dark, usually in foul weather, and at a fair speed for about 8 to 10 miles, with the fear of pursuit ever on his mind. Later in the smuggling period these human-borne kegs were refined to an elliptical section, which did go some way to alleviating the pain the ordinary tubman had to suffer.

The tubman, in countryman's smock, using a stout staff
and carrying the carefully designed elliptical barrels

Luckier than he was the pony-handler, whose stout beasts of burden
came from the great moors of Devon and Somerset as well as the New
Forest, and could carry two large barrels, and even a third atop these
slung either side. These barrels also gained an elliptical shape, making
them more manageable. The staggering tubmen, the strings of ponies and
the waggons transported the goods swiftly off the beaches, and had to be

guarded on their flanks, just as in any other military-style operation. Ambush was, of course, the greatest danger, with hot, cavalry pursuit being the other, and it was the smugglers' soldiery or 'batmen' who carried out the duty of screening their carrying comrades. They were so-called because, in the earlier days of the smuggling war, it was death to be caught assisting smugglers by carrying arms of any sort, and so instead they used the long holly-wood bats, tipped with iron ferrules, which they handled like the quarter staves Robin Hood is said to have used. Indeed, it was a similar sort of admiration which gave the smugglers so great an advantage over the forces of the Crown, for their customers were grateful to them not only for supplying them with their contraband but also for standing up to authority in the same way as Robin Hood and his merry men were supposed to have done in medieval times. The free traders made a huge contribution to keeping up the morale of the lower classes in an age when governance of the realm was very much a 'them and us' situation. Government by consensus may have flourished briefly for a few years just after the middle of the twentieth century in Britain, but in the smugglers' golden age, it was a long way off.

These, then, were the smuggling PBI (the poor bloody infantry), the unrecorded soldiers and carriers without whom the vast amounts of contraband could never have been transported from the beaches upon which it was landed by the sea-smugglers to the great markets in the towns and the individuals and small communities who eagerly awaited the goods. These anonymous smugglers were the ancestors of many of the residents of the counties which lie along the southern coasts of this country, who, usually with considerable pride, can be heard to this day remarking that their forebears were smugglers. And in many a churchyard can be found the epitaphs of smugglers, all of them carved with sympathy by the local masons. The most moving is in the churchyard in the former village of Kinson in Dorset, now part of Bournemouth, Gulliver's home, which reads:

To the memory of
Robert Trotman
Late of Rond in the County of Wilts.,
Who was barbarously murder'd on the shore near
Poole, the 24th March, 1765.

A little tea, one leaf, I did not steal.
For guiltless blood shed I to God appeal.
Put tea in one scale, human blood in t'other,
And think what 'tis to slay thy harmless brother.

William Lewis got a magnificent headstone in the graveyard of Wyke Regis, also in the county of Dorset, which shows the Revenue schooner *Pigmy* attacking Lewis's smuggling cutter:

Sacred to the memory of William Lewis, was killed by a shot from the 'Pigmy' schooner, 21st April, 1822, aged 33 years.

Of life bereft, by fell design,
I mingle with my fellow clay.
On God's protection I recline
To save me on the Judgement Day:
There shall each blood-stained soul appear:
Repent, all, ere it be too late,
Or else a dreadful doom you'll hear,
For God will soon avenge my fate . . .

This stone was erected by his Wife as the last mark of respect to an Affectionate Husband.

The second half of the eighteenth century was a time of considerable unrest in England. The main reason was the wars which Englishmen were engaged in for much of the period: as the intervals between these conflicts came round, thousands of men who had been trained to kill and made to live in the harshest conditions in army camps and ships-of-war – men who, moreover, had a deep loathing of authority driven into their minds in these places – came out of the services, and many of them went to swell the ranks of the smugglers and other outlaws.

Once they took up smuggling, joining the gangs and companies of free traders, their attitude to the authority of the state was reinforced when they saw how powerless the king's officers were to oppose, let alone prevent, their running the smuggled goods which were their stock-in-trade. They saw, too, how relatively easy smuggling was, how respected and even admired they were as they brought to all classes of people the reasonably priced goods they so much valued. Most of all, they appreciated the large amounts of money in their pockets, far more than the meagre pay they received, if they were lucky, as seamen and soldiers of the king. And if they ever had any qualms of conscience about defrauding the king of his Customs, they could tell themselves that if they were bad men as smugglers, then it was a bad law which made them so. In this way, they joined the ranks of the derelicts, tramps, deserters, cripples, gypsies, escaped convicts, bankrupts, profligates and rakes who resorted to the wastelands, forests and moors in the Weald of Kent, the New Forest and Cranborne Chase in Dorset, where they mingled and lived with the famous deer-poachers who were such a trial to the local landowners. Here they could all do a good hard job and be paid for it, out of the clutches of the Royal Navy's hated press-gang, and with a choice of trades at their fingertips: tubman, horse-leader, signaller, batman, waggoner. It was a trade in which there was the chance of making your fortune if you were bright enough, and which would continue as long as the British Empire lasted and its kings taxed its people through the imposition of so many Customs dues. Why else would the great ones of the free trade spend thousands of pounds digging out tunnels between the quays and inns of the seaports, deep under the pavements of the streets where the Customs and Excise officers walked and watched? Why else should these rich men secretly construct deep underground rooms, and build themselves fine houses with a multiplicity of cellars and secret chambers? The free trade, the smugglers comforted themselves, would last as long as commerce itself, which showed no signs of ceasing. Someone coined the phrase which summed up the country at this time as being 'an island surrounded by smugglers'.

How ironical it was, then, that the very wars which presented the smugglers with so many golden opportunities at the same time prevented the government from being able to curb their lawless trade! *The Gentlemen's Magazine* commented in 1735: 'In several parts of Kent the farmers are obliged to raise wages and yet are distressed for want of hands to get in their harvest, which is attributed to the great numbers who employ themselves in smuggling along the coast.' Clearly the Kentish smugglers were doing well right from the beginning of the eighteenth century: after all, they had had a lot of practice way back in the owling days. This sense of supremacy over other counties must have contributed in no small measure to the violent way in which they lorded it over their home grounds and maintained their reigns of terror.

By the middle of that century it was estimated that the total number of smugglers on the southern coast of England outnumbered the king's men who were supposed to oppose them (Revenue officers, Excise officers, cutter crews, and dragoons and other cavalry) by ten to one. It would seem like unfair odds in any conflict; this one could justifiably be looked upon as the second English civil war.

The war against the smugglers erupted every now and again into pitched battles. These did not necessarily involve large forces on either side, but their ferocity and the fact that they took place at all was outrageous in a land which in theory enjoyed the king's peace. The Battle of Hook's Wood, the Seige of Goudhurst and the Battle of Milford Green have already been mentioned; in 1784 another very serious affray took place in Hampshire – the Battle of Mudeford. This was during the period of William Arnold's term of office as collector of Customs at Cowes in the Isle of Wight. The local smugglers were growing bolder and bolder as 1784 wore on: in June the *Swan* Revenue cutter had been attacked by smugglers, who had disarmed the preventers and taken from them twelve pistols, nine cutlasses and four muskets. Arnold had to ask his masters in London to send replacement weapons. In July the collector got a tipoff about a large run which the smugglers were planning in the vicinity of that notorious smuggling town, Christchurch. Arnold had been nagging London for a Royal Navy frigate to be sent to patrol both Christchurch and Poole bays, but all the Admiralty would give him was HM sloop-of-war *Orestes*, a yellow-painted, ship-rigged vessel of 300 tons with eighteen guns, and having ports in her sides through which sweeps could be deployed for work in shallow water. Captain Ellis, her commander, agreed to use Studland Bay in the Isle of Purbeck as his base, and Arnold issued him and his officers with special warrants called 'deputations', which gave them the same powers as Customs officers to search and seize at sea. Captain Ellis proved to be an apt smuggler-fighter, and he had several successes under his belt by the time his real test arrived.

Hurst Castle, King Henry VIII's gun-fort which guarded the entrance to the Solent, was at this time a neglected place, shamefully left to rot and infested by a nest of smugglers, led by a vicious character called John Streeter. (Quite why Arnold allowed the situation at Hurst to continue is something of a mystery which has not been solved to this day.) It was pretty certain that Streeter was leading the run of which Arnold had been warned, and that two luggers were to be expected. Arnold had alerted Captain Ellis of the *Orestes* and Captain Sarmon of the cutter *Swan*, and when Ellis was informed that the run had started he made for Mudeford just outside Christchurch, where the two rivers Stour and Avon debouch as one into Christchurch Bay through a narrow channel known as the Run. Ellis found an Excise cutter had beaten him to it, the captain of which had entered the Run to find the two luggers anchored just inside the harbour.

Captain Sarmon saw a huge crowd of people on the shore and so landed to find out what was going on. He was told that the previous afternoon the two smuggling vessels had landed a huge quantity of tea and assorted spirits, which had needed fifty waggons and three hundred horses to shift from the beach, in which Herculean task the people present had been more than a little involved. Sarmon even saw some of the cargo still on the beach, due for collection that very day, the huge transport force having been unable to cope with it the day before. The Excise captain, with only a few of the very small number of crew from his very small cutter to protect him, went straight to the smuggled packages with the intention of seizing them in the name of the king; but the people of Christchurch and its environs made threatening gestures and noises, which the brave Excise officer took to mean that they weren't going to allow him to seize their goods in the king's or anyone else's name. Furious, Sarmon tried to go on board the anchored luggers, but again his way was barred by the ugly mob. Sarmon saw he was bested, went back to his cutter and went out to sea to meet the *Swan* and the *Orestes*. Together they went into the beach, a small but determined squadron of the king's ships.

One could be forgiven for believing that this force and the authority it carried would have overawed the people on shore, but this was not the case. They simply stood and watched what the sailors would do next. When a little way off the shore, Captain Ellis of the *Orestes* lowered a boat crewed by armed sailors and under the command of his sailing master, a young officer named William Allen. This boat rowed up through the Run, closely followed by the two cutters; but as the long boat neared the upper end of the channel a shot rang out, closely followed by a veritable fusillade from both the two anchored luggers and from the windows of the Haven House Inn which overlooked the Run. The smugglers, up to that point invisible, also fired upon the king's vessels from a breastwork at the top of the beach.

Allen was immediately hit, and the cutters opened fire in reply with their six-pounders. The smugglers continued to fire and Allen was hit again, this time fatally, but the rowing-boat continued to make for the luggers in the teeth of the hail of fire from the miscreants. Reaching their objectives, the sailors leaped aboard both vessels and seized them, although not before the crews in them had disembarked. Before the cutters' crews were able to get ashore, the smugglers had run off taking the sails with them. The Revenue men towed the luggers off and sailed them out of the harbour; prize-crews were put aboard the smuggling ships by Captain Ellis and off they went in the direction of Cowes.

Collector William Arnold wrote in his report of the grave incident to his masters on the Board of Customs in London:

> An inquest has been held on the body of Mr. Allen, and the jury have returned a verdict of wilful murder; the coroner has issued a warrant for apprehending William Parrott and William May, two persons who were proved to have been accessories to the murder.
>
> None of the rest are known or discovered, but the transaction having happened in the face of day and so near Christchurch, it is more than probable that many of the persons assembled on the spot must be known in the neighbourhood. We have judged it necessary to write to Mr. Jeans, Supervisor of Riding Officers at Christchurch, to excite him to use his endeavours to apprehend the offenders.
>
> A report having gone about that before the new Act for preventing smuggling comes into force, an Act of Oblivion for all smuggling offences will be passed, we are fully persuaded that they are induced to act in a more daring and desperate manner under an idea – but a mistaken one, we hope – that all offences against the Revenue or outrages on officers will be pardoned.

May and Parrott escaped prosecution, but another smuggler called Coombes was convicted of the murder of Sailing Master William Allen of HM sloop-of-war *Orestes*, and he was ordered to be hanged on

> the gallows set and placed in the public stream in the River of Thames within the flush of the sea and water and jurisdiction of our Admiralty before the bank called Wapping on Monday the 23rd January. The said George Coombes, at the influx of the sea and water, there you are to hang [him] by the neck until he shall be dead according to the maritime customs observed . . . And that you are, immediately after the execution, to take the body of the said George Coombes to be hung in chains at some conspicuous place on the coast of Kent or Essex . . . Given under the Great Seal of the High Court of Admiralty.

The court also ordered that the body be dissected and anatomized, and must have assumed that Coombes was one of the notorious Kentish smugglers, which indicates how associated they were in the public mind with such outrages as the Battle of Mudeford and the murder of a Royal Navy officer. However, once Coombes had been dispatched, orders came to take the corpse to Mudeford, where it was hung in an iron body-cage from a gibbet erected on Haven Point because the crime he had committed had been carried out there. Coombes's body did not hang rotting for long: one night it was taken down and given a secret Christian burial.

William Arnold revealed that he had 'judged it necessary to write to Mr. Jeans, Supervisor of Riding Officers at Christchurch, to excite him to use his endeavours to apprehend the offenders'. It is doubtful whether this did much good, even though Jeans was Arnold's subordinate, for Jeans soon became the subject of an inquiry by his masters, the Board of Customs. Mr Monday, general surveyor of Customs, was sent down, and in the report he made on his investigation, dated May 1786, he revealed that before 1784 Jeans had on several occasions failed to support and assist his riding officers and had actively discouraged them from doing their duty, this after senior Customs officers had had to order them to attend more thoroughly to their duty! It transpired that just before the day of the battle these conscientious officers had actually seen the smugglers' waggons being driven through the town and out to

Mudeford. They had reported this activity to Jeans, together with their suspicion that a huge run was about to be made, and had asked him for his orders. The supervisor replied that it was his considered opinion that they should go home to bed, for that was just what he was going to do!

As Monday also discovered, Jeans had been in the habit of forbidding his riding officers to enter in their official journals the names and descriptions of smuggling vessels which they had observed off their coast, a duty which they were strictly enjoined to carry out by the printed instructions on every page of those journals (see p. 34). After the Battle of Mudeford Jeans had actually forbidden his men to make any reference to the episode, which had culminated in the death of William Allen. And on the day itself he had told them to keep away from Mudeford.

As soon as the commissioners read Monday's report they dismissed Jeans from the service and the career of the four-times mayor of Christchurch was finished.

It may be thought from what has been said so far about the type of people who followed the free trade that only men were involved. However, this was not the case. Granted, no woman was physically strong enough to run contraband in the usual way, but in the hiding of items and the actual transportation of such goods as silks and satins they did much useful work. Perhaps the most famous was Lovey Warne, the sister of two smugglers who guarded the junction of several vital smuggling-paths in the New Forest. A pretty young woman, she was in the habit of trotting off on her New Forest pony to the nearest port when she knew certain quite legitimate coasting vessels were to be tied up at the quay; once there she would go aboard and make her way down to the captain's cabin. Having been greeted by the captain, she would strip off all her clothes, take the end of a length of costly silk, satin or lace, hold it to her waist, and then twirl round and round until she was girdled by the luxurious contraband. Then she would dress herself, put on her voluminous plaid shawl, take her farewell of her grateful friend the captain, and climb carefully back onto the quay. There she would smile coyly at any Customs men who might have been watching her movements, and trip across the cobbles back to her waiting pony, which would carry her back to her brothers in their cottage-cum-warehouse, safe in the great fastness of the New Forest.

Lovey Warne smuggling lace and silks

Lovey also played a vital part in the smugglers' warning-system in this area: when pony-trains were toiling along the forest tracks near her home and there was an immediate threat to their safety from Customs men who were getting too close for comfort, Lovey would go to the top of the highest hill in that stretch of the New Forest and unfurl the bright red cloak which she wore for the purpose. She could thus be seen for miles, a living danger-signal, as long as danger lasted. She was remembered for years after her death for the way in which, when quite advanced in years, she would tuck up her skirts and make off along the smugglers' paths on her sure-footed New Forest pony with a bottle of brandy balanced on either side of her waist and suspended from her stout leather belt.

Lovey Warne takes her place beside the hundreds of smugglers' women who gamely assisted in the free trade: the 'bumboat women' in the great harbours who went aboard the merchant ships and stuffed silks and satins into their clothing and poured spirits into the belly-canteens under their skirts and then smuggled the goods ashore; the female 'duffers' who marched along the roads from the south and east coasts with their canvas, tea-stuffed overcoats; and the rest of the unknown women who smuggled goods in a hundred secret ways.

The main island of the British Isles is but the largest of many, and the very much smaller islands each posed a particular and peculiar problem both for the smuggler and his opposite number in the king's forces. Some islands were outside the direct rule of the British government and ruled themselves, while others were so small and so remote that they were almost impossible to govern.

The greatest advantage of an island is that it is surrounded by water, which, as John of Gaunt pointed out,

> . . . serves it in the office of a wall,
> Or as a moat defensive to a house,
> Against the envy of less happier lands . . .

The smugglers on the smaller islands of the British Isles were always on the lookout to ensure that 'the coast was clear' for their sea-colleagues coming in to land their contraband.

The Isle of Man was one of the finest bases for smuggling, with its ancient independence and laws, its sovereign parliament and its geographical position between Ireland, Scotland and England. On the isle itself centuries of lore and legend, mainly about giants, witches and ghosts, were used by the smugglers to safeguard their hides if they ever needed to. However, it was the Isle of Man's fiscal laws which were the focus of the free traders who used it, not all of whom were native Manxmen. Lace, tobacco, tea, wines and spirits needed to have no duty paid on them when they were brought by ship on to the isle, and it was the wily merchants of nearby Liverpool, one of the greatest ports and commercial centres in the kingdom, who saw the possibilities of such a situation. They proceeded to build up the import trade so that, like the provident citizens of the Channel Islands, they would have plenty of warehouses full of potential contraband for the smugglers. The Isle of Man's capital, Douglas, had its port installations vastly improved through the munificence of the Liverpudlian entrepreneurs: great quays were built for the merchant ships bringing goods into the isle as well as for the smugglers' vessels, mostly heavily armed luggers and cutters, which would take the cargoes, now as contraband, across the sea to the southern coasts of Scotland and the English coasts of Cumberland. Once the contraband had landed it was taken on into the Lake District by smugglers who also trafficked in illicit whisky made in the hundreds of stills in the area, each one at the mercy of the local Excise officers, for 'moonshine' was their particular concern. Certainly, once contraband, whether from outside or inside the Lake District, was in the hands of the smugglers, pursuit was made very difficult because of the mountainous nature of the terrain, the unreliable weather conditions and the ingenuity of the smugglers, who knew every path and hiding-place. Smugglers' huts, caves, quarries, empty tombs and even family vaults in the churchyards were all pressed into service in this particular theatre of the constant war throughout the kingdom between smuggler and king's officer.

After 1765 when the lord of Man sold his prerogatives to the British Crown, salt alone was still allowed into the Isle of Man for the continued curing of the world-famous Manx herrings and kippers. Naturally, the smugglers' merchants took in far more salt than this vital industry actually needed and sold it to the smugglers, who made large profits from its resale, since salt was still big business, heavily taxed as it was by most countries.[5]

South of the Isle of Man lies another island which was heavily used by smugglers. Lundy Island lies at the entrance to the Bristol Channel, and is very rocky. But however inhospitable it was, pirates, privateers and, of course, smugglers found it ideal for their nefarious purposes at various times in its history, lying as it does some 12 miles north-west of Hartland Point on the Devon coast.

In smuggling days its greatest user was one Thomas Benson, who in 1739 inherited from his father, on his death, the family's trading business, together with the fine fleet of ships which was part and parcel of the Benson empire. One of the ships in the fleet which he inherited was to Thomas rather more than an honest merchantman: it had been licensed as a privateer and fitted out with twenty guns and the men to serve them, and was named *The Benson Galley*, though it was not propelled by oars. With this fleet the Bensons traded with Canada, the colonies in America, France, Portugal and many places in the

Mediterranean Sea. With such worldwide trade it was fairly inevitable that sooner or later little Lundy Island would fall under the commercial aegis of the ambitious Benson family.

The Benson business prospered under the new director, and in 1746 Thomas was appointed sheriff of the county of Devonshire; a year later he became Member of Parliament for the constituency of Barnstaple. Here was approbation indeed, not only in his home county but in the very seat of government and the heart of the nation. Now Thomas was specializing in the tobacco trade with America, for his home port of Barnstaple saw more of the trade than any other port in the kingdom, save London. Then Benson suddenly broadened the scope of his interests even more, for he obtained a franchise for transporting convicts to the penal colonies in America. The friends and contacts he had made through his appointments in London must have put in several good words for him. Soon Benson's ships were taking convicts out to the plantations of Virginia and bringing back the finest product of that part of the world: tobacco, the best in the trade.

Benson's next commercial step was to rent the island of Lundy from its owner, Lord Gower. So it was that many of the convicts on Benson's ships found themselves setting foot, not in the New World, but on a rocky islet at the opening of the Bristol Channel, a mere 12 miles from Bideford, but well outside British territorial waters. They were soon set to work: adapting and fitting out the caves of the island as storehouses that would take the Benson tobacco, uncustomed and uncommonly good. To this day one of the most impressive caverns on Lundy bears the name Benson's Cave. The convicts acted as the dockers and porters, heaving the great hogsheads up the cliffs to the stores, where more convicts divided up the larger parcels of tobacco into smaller ones, all ready and convenient for smuggling into the mainland areas just across the sea in Devon and Somerset, to say nothing of the more dangerous runs up the great River Avon and into the port of Bristol itself.

Like most smugglers, Thomas Benson ran into trouble. In 1740 the Customs men stopped his ship *Grace*, rummaged through her and found tobacco, so much, in fact, that when he was found guilty the fine was a massive £922. In the following year the Customs officers, now hot on the trail, caught him again and again, until Thomas Benson, sheriff of the county of Devonshire and Member of Parliament, owed the king

£8,319 after defrauding him of his Customs. Benson decided to fight the case, for he was sure that 'the law's delays' would lead to the action dragging on and on, and, being an optimist, he hoped that something would turn up and that he would once more be in funds; failing that, one of the friends he had in London might be able to help him out of the mess in which he now found himself.

All went well until 1751 when the Customs authorities in Devon decided they had to act and made a visit to Lundy Island, tipped off by someone who wished Benson ill. Sure enough, they discovered traces of the tobacco manufactory, but there was not enough evidence to mount another case, for Benson himself had been tipped off and had had the isle cleared of the incriminating trade, lock, stock and barrel, as well as the convict-workers. Benson was thoroughly scared by this raid on 'his island', but more so by the fact that some of the convicts could not be accounted for, and he could only assume that they had escaped to the mainland where they now posed a threat with all the incriminating information they were capable of placing before the authorities.

Thomas Benson was in a tight spot and so he used desperate measures to get out of it. He heavily insured the oldest ship in his fleet, loaded her to the gunwales with a mixed cargo of miscellaneous items and sent her out from Bideford. Her complement was a motley collection of no-goods and convicts, both male and female, who were shackled together. The captain of this desperate venture, under Benson's direct orders, of course, took the ship out into the Atlantic 50 miles west of Lundy, where he set fire to and scuttled her. Both he and the crew managed to take to the boats and eventually came ashore at Clovelly. Here, after a short interval, the bosun turned informer against Benson and Customs were called in. The insurance fraud involved more and more officials putting together the case against Benson, but again Customs were ahead of the other creditors and they served Benson with yet another demand, this time for £6,187 in settlement of his outstanding debt. However, Benson had had enough: he took a ship to Portugal, where he had strong commercial connections, and he decided to stay there, permanently.

In 1754 the officers of the scuttled ship were put on trial in the Court of Admiralty in London. The wretched captain was found guilty of firing and scuttling his ship in the execution of the insurance fraud; he was hanged at Execution Dock on the River Thames. The law officers had been trying to extradite Benson from Portugal, but he escaped all their efforts by disappearing over the border into Spain, where he remained until things had died down again. Then he returned to Portugal where, from his last home, he continued to trade using the last remaining ship of what had once been a proud fleet of Devonshire craft, the only vessel he had been able to keep. At length, in 1771, after a long career of commerce, fraud and smuggling, Thomas Benson died peacefully in his bed in exile, but in a land he loved.[6]

Southwards round the coast of Cornwall from Lundy and just off Land's End lie the Isles of Scilly. Jesse Mothersole, in her monumental book on the island group called *The Isles of Scilly; their story, their folk, their flowers*, published in 1910, wrote:

Smuggling was a very popular employment. It was so easy to slip over to France and return with a cargo of contraband goods, which could be dropped overboard attached to a buoy if the revenue–officer inconveniently appeared. Even the clergy engaged in the traffic. It is said that Parson Troutbeck, who speaks feelingly of the drunkenness occasioned by smuggling, was himself obliged to leave the islands from fear of the consequences of having taken part in it. The Parsonage on Tresco was originally built in a spot especially convenient for this trade, although not otherwise suitable; and one of its tenants had also to run way because he was mixed up in some smuggling affair.

With a hundred and forty islands in the group and some of the most dangerous rocks, shoals and ledges in the world between them, the smugglers of Scilly had to be among the finest seamen in the world. This and the utter remoteness of the group from any seat of government administration made collecting Customs and Excise levies a virtual impossibility. Exacerbating all this was the weather, which could always cut the island group off from the mainland for months at a time. In smuggling days there was no regular communication with England, which was both an advantage and a disadvantage. For centuries the Scillonians had to rely entirely on their own efforts for survival, through kelping, fishing, piloting big merchantmen coming up the Channel, and, of course, smuggling. The danger of famine was ever present, their crops might fail and their staple occupations might be affected by misfortune.

Today each of the larger islands in the group keeps its own gig, a long four- or six-man rowing boat, narrow and with clean classical lines. In smuggling days these were used for high-speed runs across to Britanny, for they could be whipped through the water at well over 10 knots. Each gig could carry only a limited amount of cargo back home, but it was enough for the islanders' humble needs, consisting, as it did, mainly of liquor which the crews and their families proceeded to use to excess, thereby giving rise to the legends of drunkenness for which the islands were notorious. So hard and grim was life on the islands, particularly in the winter, that the inhabitants needed all the rum and brandy they could smuggle just to get through the bitterly cold season of storms, when they would be cut off from the mainland for long periods.

The Customs house on the main island, St Mary's, was built as early as 1696 because the deputy-governor had suddenly realized how much smuggling was going on and was alarmed that his efficiency would be called into question. Tea, brandy and rum were the staple contraband of the smugglers of the Scilly Isles, almost all of which they needed for themselves, but they did traffic in more exotic goods, which they obtained from the great ships of the East India Company as they passed the isles. Once spotted by the lookouts on the outer islands the gigs would be rushed into the water and the race would be on. The winner got the contract for guiding the great ship on up the Channel, while the rest of his crew and those of the other gigs started the real business of bargaining with the sailors of the merchant ship over the smuggled goods as it sailed past the lethal rocks of the Scilly Isles, safely piloted by a skilled Scillonian. Spices, jewellery and kerchiefs of the finest oriental silk were the main items, for they took up little space in the gigs as they were rowed back to the islands. Once there, the same boats would take the contraband on to such ports as Penzance and St Ives, as well as a hundred beaches up and down the Cornish coast. So it was that the wives and sweethearts of that remote county received the latest in silks from the smugglers long before the ladies of London and even Bath, those centres of eighteenth-century culture and fashion. In this way the Scilly Isles were regarded as the clearing-house for fancy goods in the great days of smuggling.

The wars against Napoleon, which raged from 1793, with a short interval, until the Battle of Waterloo brought them to an end in 1815, had, in fact, a very debilitating effect on the islands, just as they had on the rest of Britain, of course. However, with such a fragile and quirky economy the Scilly Isles felt this effect more keenly than most parts of the kingdom. Though it had first been established to deal with the rapacious smugglers of the counties of Kent and Sussex, the coastal blockade, set up while the French wars were still on, had a severe effect upon the smugglers of the Scilly Isles. So serious was the impact of the anti-smuggling measures on the islanders' staple trade of smuggling that, when it was severely curtailed, real poverty was diagnosed among the population. Their perilous plight came to the notice of the civil authorities on the mainland, in itself a clear indication of how severe it was, with the result that in 1818, just three years after the end of the wars against the French, a party of magistrates crossed over the sea from the nearest mainland town, Penzance, in order to look into the state and causes of the Scillonians' plight, and to find, if they could, some means of relieving it. In the report they eventually published they named the causes as the shortage of corn (growing it was hard because the islands were so rocky and lacking in soil), together with the fact that the harvests of the previous two years had failed; the failure, too, of the kelp crops; the decline in piloting opportunities because the 'Branch Pilots', an official organization, had recently been established; the partial failure of the ling fishery; and finally, and most importantly, though the magistrates could hardly have put this first and foremost in their report, the suppression of smuggling into, out of and between the Scilly Isles. The latter was the result of the work of the highly successful Preventive Service, which had used the ships, boats and skilled ex-Royal Navy crews, as well as the military organization instituted by the high command of the new service. The islanders, concluded the magistrates from Penzance, had been deprived of their chief means of supporting themselves and their families.

Directly the report was made public throughout the kingdom, a countrywide public subscription fund was set up, and the government sent experts in the fishing industry to the Scilly Isles so that their fishing activities could be revived to a level which would bring subsistence income to the men of the island group. This was the only way, for smuggling was in terminal decline, and by 1840 the trade was as good as dead.[7]

The Channel Islands, or *Les Iles Anglo-Normandes*, enjoyed a similar status to that of the Isle of Man, and the smugglers were not slow to appreciate this. After the lord of Man sold his rights in that island to the Crown in 1765, the Manx smugglers and the merchants who supplied them had to look elsewhere, for the Customs service moved in and imposed its law. Their eyes turned southwards and lighted upon the Channel Islands. The English smugglers had always used this offshore group, but now the free trade was ready to expand dramatically. Being under the British Crown they are, nevertheless, self-governing by their own parliaments and the laws these pass; in addition, unless specially signified, the Channel Islands are not bound by British Acts of Parliament, although the British government is responsible, nevertheless, for the defence of the islands and for foreign relations. The Channel Islands were part of the duchy of Normandy and they comprise the only part of that duchy still held by the British Crown. This unique position ensured for the smugglers and their suppliers a freedom from Customs law which made the Channel Islands even more attractive for the free trade than the Isle of Man; there were also more islands in the group. Huge warehouses were stuffed with potential contraband from France and other countries, and the special containers so prized by the English smugglers were developed here: oilskin teabags on Jersey, and the elliptical barrels with their neat harnesses on Guernsey.

The merchants of the Channel Islands, both British settlers and native, prized the English smugglers above all their customers for they ensured that the economy of the Islands was second to none in Europe. Therefore, the governments of these very fortunate isles did all they could to encourage and maintain the illicit trade, for which they had become the most important entrepôt. Interference with the free trade was, when necessary, actively discouraged by the authorities of the islands: from time to time it was not uncommon for the soldiers in the forts on the northern shores of the most northerly of the islands to open fire on British Revenue and even Royal Navy cruisers when they were seen by the watchers on the shore to be crossing the boundary of the islands' territorial waters in pursuit of smuggling vessels. These ships may have simply been doing their job by chasing the king's enemies in this smuggling war, but when they threatened Channel Islands' sovereignty, and the Channel Islands' smugglers too, then the guns under the Union

The Haven, as the Channel Islands were known for most of the period of
English smuggling

flag on the fort had no hesitation in firing on king's ships flying the same
Union flag.

Such an anomalous situation could not be allowed to continue
indefinitely; it was a wonder how it managed to last so long. It took a
very hard-fought campaign in Parliament at Westminster for the
government to force through the legislation necessary to bring the
Channel Islands into line with the rest of the king's realm as far as
Customs law was concerned. The first move took place in 1802 when
the signing of the Peace of Amiens brought a halt to the war with
France, albeit only a temporary lull as it transpired. In that year Customs
commissioners were sent to the Channel Islands and received a frosty
reception. On the island of Guernsey, for example, the merchants who
employed the hundreds of coopers making the special smuggling barrels
had had to dismiss their craftsmen in order to prevent their discovery by
the commissioners. When the commissioners landed on the island itself
these merchants met them at the quayside in a demonstration of protest
which became so heated that it had to be broken up by the soldiers of
the island's garrison on the orders of the governor. The merchants even
had to be escorted back to their palatial homes, while still protesting at
the commissioners' visit.

The main point which the protesters had been trying to put to the
men from London was that practically everyone was involved in
smuggling in one way or another, either supplying goods or moving

them, equipping or provisioning the smugglers, and that if the free trade was suppressed there would be no other form of work from which the islanders could continue to gain a livelihood. The second point made by the merchants was that such a suppression would, in fact, form an infringement of the constitution of the Channel Islands. However, the commissioners were able to counter these startling claims by stating firmly that the smugglers of the Channel Islands were currently, at what was a time of war or had been not many months before, depriving the Crown of well over a million pounds sterling each year, quite apart from the damage they were doing to the British war effort when they smuggled spies, dispatches, escaped prisoners and golden guineas.

Soon after this visit the Channel Islands were brought into line with the rest of the kingdom's Customs and Excise laws, and the outraged merchants of the islands demanded huge sums of money by way of compensation from the government in London. The Customs houses were built on the islands while the wars against the French were still being fought, that is before the final victory for the allies in 1815. While this was happening the smugglers moved their homes, and their merchants their businesses lock, stock and barrel to such French ports as Cherbourg and Roscoff. With the new scientific age that had dawned, the English smugglers could no longer enjoy the unique facilities of the Channel Islands.[8]

In 1799 the Isle of Wight was said to be almost a century behind the rest of the kingdom. Its small population, offshore situation and lack of industry rendered it virtually worthless to the nation; its only real value was in wartime as a military area. However, for the smugglers, at that apogee of their craft, the Isle of Wight was a unique geographical feature which gave them opportunities and challenges not found in any other part of the country, be it mainland or island.

The small population, the scattered farms and dwellings, the lack of many great houses and the distances between what few villages there were made the islanders very glad of the contraband, usually smuggled from Cherbourg, a mere 60 or so miles from the southernmost tip of the island. However, it was as a staging-post for contraband that it was most useful to the smugglers. Along the two southern coastal stretches of this diamond-shaped island the men of the villages did not bother to dabble in fishing: they devoted themselves to smuggling. They received the goods, landed them, stored them and then sorted them into loads for onward transportation in easy stages northwards across the island to the northern coasts, where they would be taken in quite small boats either across Spithead to secret landing-places in the great harbour of Portsmouth, or across the Solent to the coasts of Hampshire and Dorset.

Running contraband on to the southern coast of the Isle of Wight needed courage and the very highest standards of seamanship, for powerful currents, double tides, treacherous winds and rocky ledges just below the surface of the sea, second only to those of the Scilly Isles in their lethal power to wreck ships, made it one of the most dangerous landfalls in the British Isles. There were no ports or harbours worth speaking of on these south-facing coasts for these reasons, and the smugglers welcomed this fact, but the high cliffs and narrow beaches, with few chines or ravines up which to take the contraband, made their work very difficult. At sea, captains, whether they were Revenue, Royal Navy or smuggling, had to know the waters round this part of the Wight very well indeed, and few in number were the king's ships who chased a smuggler in close, for the advantage was always with the latter.

The smugglers of the Isle of Wight went on smuggling long after the practice had died out in the rest of the country: in 1869 the poet Sidney Dobell was holidaying at Niton at the southernmost tip of the island and wrote: 'The whole population here are smugglers! Everyone has an ostensible occupation, but nobody gets his money by it, or cares to work in it. Here are fishermen who never fish, but always have pockets full of money, and farmers whose farming consists of ploughing the deep at night, and whose daily time is spent in standing like herons on lookout-posts.'

This was nothing new: the surprise was in the length of time it had continued. In 1748, for instance, *The Westminster Journal* for 23 January stated: 'We hear from the New Forest in Hampshire that the Smugglers have got to such a height in that part of the country that scarce a week passes but great quantities of goods are run between Lymington and Christchurch, which is attributed to the want of the usual guard at the Needles, it having of late been surprisingly neglected.'

William Arnold was similarly alarmed when he took up his post as Collector of Customs at Cowes in 1777, writing to those who had appointed him of the impudent smugglers of the Isle of Wight and the Hampshire coasts, and the dangerously powerful ships they were building. However, these expressions of alarm at the neglect by central government are typical of the long war against the smugglers, with the sporadic efforts of some minister being followed by a slackening of resolve as new ministers followed, instead of high-profile measures being consistently implemented at all levels to break the smugglers, both on land and at sea, and kill off their menace to the health of the nation once and for all. The Isle of Wight, in fact, epitomized in its small scale the problems of this period.

As men like Arnold got to grips with the smuggling situation, so the smugglers of the Wight stepped up their efforts on the southern coasts and scaled down their operations on the northern. And on the eastern tip of the island it was the port of Bembridge which became an active scene of smuggling, for here the contrabandists used 14 ft gigs on their trips across the Channel to the ports of Cherbourg and Harfleur. Each of these custom-built rowing-boats could carry twenty tubs of spirits, which was a modest but at the same time profitable cargo. Indeed, the rows of substantial cottages which are such an attractive feature of this little port were built almost entirely on the proceeds of such trips to France. The Bembridge windmill was a fine lookout-post for the smugglers, of the sort mentioned by the poet Dobell, as well as a signal-station for their boats and ships, the sails being used like semaphore arms, and as a distinctive sea-mark for vessels, both legal and illegal.

The Isle of Wight even had a few gangs, so much was it a true microcosm of the smuggling situation all along the southern coasts of England. One of the most notorious was the Mottistone Gang from the village of that name on the south-west coast of the island. The village has a fine church which was used both as store and seamark by the smugglers, and in the graveyard is a large family tomb which was used for hiding small orders of contraband for short periods while awaiting collection by customers living close to the church. The Mottistone Gang also used the caves in the cliffs just above the beach, and from the nearby row of cottages signals were sent to incoming ships through the small windows, like eyes both watching and warning. Many Isle of Wight cottages were ideally placed for this type of work, the watchers in front of such dwellings giving warning to those inside who watched the sea when danger, in the form of searching king's officers, came along the street and up to the front doors.[9]

The shears was a crane used by the smugglers of Beachy
Head, Sussex, to haul up contraband from the beach
while their enemies were changing from beach to cliff
patrol as the tide came in. On this occasion a 'Warrior'
fell into the basket and was promptly hauled up by the
smugglers. Reaching the top, he fired his pistol to warn
his mates and the smugglers ran off, leaving him with the
contraband of best brandy

As a result of the very high cliffs around much of the Isle of Wight, special methods had to be evolved to raise smuggled goods up off the beaches that had no convenient cutting in the rockface. In much the same way as the smugglers of the Isle of Purbeck in nearby Dorset, who had the same cliffs to contend with, the smugglers of the Isle of Wight had to use shear-legs as well as single stakes driven into the cliffs up which to haul baskets, and in some cases five-barred field-gates, up from the beaches with the smuggled goods either in or on them.

The Wight's remoteness may have had the effect of slackening the efficiency of the Coast Guard, once it had been formed, if the following incident is anything to go by. A Coast Guard court of inquiry, which opened on 22 February 1836, heard that on the previous Christmas Day a battle had taken place between smugglers and coast guards on the beach of Totland Bay. When the coast guards realized they were outnumbered by a far superior force they sent rocket signals to the nearest station asking for help. While the fight raged, a smuggling ship came in and landed contraband.

The accused was the commander of the Freshwater Coast Guard station, Lieutenant Josiah Durnford, RN, who was charged with colluding with smugglers, accepting bribes from them, falsifying his reports, and several other very serious matters. It turned out that Durnford had on that Christmas Day given his men several bottles of rum each, had ordered them to sit snugly by their fire in the watch-hut, and ignore the half-past four in the afternoon start to their patrol. Durnford in his defence asserted that there was no proof that smuggled goods had been landed on the beach while the fight was in progress, and that the spirits he had given to his men by way of Christmas presents had been very well watered. Also, with the weather being so foul, he had thought the men would not need to go outside for, with such a heavy sea running, he had been sure that no attempt would be made by the smugglers to land their contraband. However, it was all to no avail: witnesses assured the court that Durnford seldom, if ever, did night-duty and that his men were frequently drunk and incapable of their duty, while one witness claimed that a well-known and notorious smuggler had an arrangement with the coast guard commander whereby he paid Durnford £10 for every hundred tubs of spirits he was able to land successfully.

Not surprisingly, Lieutenant Durnford left the service soon afterwards.[10]

CHAPTER SIX

WAR WITHIN WAR

With the start of the wars against Napoleon in 1793 smuggling increased immediately. Customs duties rose sharply to pay for the materials of war and the importation of all French goods was totally forbidden. To the smugglers' great delight another factor in their favour was added: all Royal Naval ships and many Revenue cutters were needed for the war effort. The smugglers had never had it so good and they knew it, especially as duties, already high at the opening of hostilities, continued to spiral upwards as the long war dragged on. Large areas of the coastal counties were virtually stripped of anti-smuggling forces, for the dragoons and other units had all been withdrawn leaving only the highly ineffectual riding officers and a few Customs rowing-boats to cope with the smugglers. It is true that a floating Home Guard was set up: the 'Sea Fencibles'. They were fishermen who were given weapons to use in their smacks in the case of invasion by Napoleon, but they were no threat to the free traders as they were smugglers too, licensed by the foolish government to bear the arms which that same government had kindly given them!

Napoleon liked the English smugglers very much indeed: when he was a prisoner on St Helena he revealed, in conversation with his gaolers, that:

The smugglers did great mischief to your government. During the war all the information I received from England came through the smugglers. They are people who have the courage and ability to do anything for money. They had, at first, a part of Dunkirk allotted to them, and at one time there were upwards of five hundred of them there. They were restricted to that quarter, but as they latterly went out of their limits, committed riots and insulted everybody, I ordered Gravelines to be prepared for their reception, where they had a little camp for their accommodation. I had every information I wanted from them. They brought over newspapers and dispatches from the spies that we had in London. They took over spies from France, landed them, and kept them in their houses for many days, dispersed them over the country, and then brought them back when they wanted. They assisted French prisoners to escape from England. The relations of these French prisoners in your country were accustomed to go to Dunkirk and Gravelines to make a bargain with them to bring over their relatives. . . . They are 'genti terribili'!

He also talked of the golden guineas which the smugglers brought over on the infamous 'guinea-run', admitting that they were 'brought over to France by the English smugglers. Even for the equipping of my last expedition after my return from Elba, a great part of the money was raised in London. . . .'[1] The point was that the price of gold had soared as the eighteenth century drew to its close through devaluation and the effects of war, and after the severe financial crisis of 1789 it was also scarce as a commodity. The result of this was that the French government became eager to get hold of as many gold English sovereigns and guineas as they could, simply because coin gold was of the purest metal. Therefore Napoleon offered 30s. for every golden English guinea, and so the English smugglers immediately started running them. They designed boats specifically for this traffic, the most shameful they were ever to embark upon; before long they were running over £10,000 in gold coins to Napoleon each week. The men of Deal in Kent were the outstanding guinea-smugglers, which is not surprising for of all the English free traders they had least reason to feel loyalty to the government, a lack of patriotism which stemmed from the day William Pitt, the prime minister, ordered his troops to seize their boats on their beach and put them all to the torch. Another place which was a centre for the guinea-run was Christchurch in Dorset, a notorious hotbed of all types of smuggling, but known today for the Black House at the entrance to the harbour which was the building where guinea-boats were actually constructed. Today this building is of the same colour, which it is originally supposed to have acquired on the day the king's officers surrounded it and smoked out the shipbuilders-cum-smugglers who were inside.

During the Anglo-French wars it was estimated that between forty and fifty ships went into Flushing each week with contraband, and on

A spy being taken across the Channel by a smuggler

them the port commandant levied a tax of 6d. per cask of spirits which they took out. Ships like these used sets of Dutch and Prussian flags and the ship's papers to go with them. The smugglers would have assumed foreign names, and men skilled in the required tongue would be on hand for when the vessels were boarded and examined at sea by the Royal Navy or Customs service.

Napoleon was extremely grateful to the English smugglers for the ten thousand guineas which were ferried from the Channel ports, and which came into the mint in Paris, under heavy escort, every week. Without this gold, it is said, the French Empire would have been unable to remain solvent. However, it was not only guineas the English smugglers took over: they carried up-to-the-minute reports to the French military authorities. Indeed, during the Peninsular War, when British forces under Arthur Wellesley were fighting the French in Portugal and Spain, Napoleon first heard of Marshal Massena's attack on the lines of Torres Vedras not from his own sources but from an English guinea-smuggler who had been told the news in England. Port installations, coastal defences, the disposition of troops standing by to repel invasion, and ship movements of all kinds: who better than some of the most experienced seamen in the world, the English smugglers, to see these things and report them back to their French masters? Did they not, as Napoleon affirmed, have 'the courage and ability to do anything for money'? By the same token, it must be pointed out, there were double-agents among the smugglers: in that way they got double the danger but double the money. It was very good pay and, if it were needed after the wars, a free pardon for all their smuggling might be available from a grateful and not too inquisitive government.

Lest it be thought that HM ships took no part in the continuing war, or rather 'armed truce', with the smugglers, it should be noted that some of the fiercest battles took place at sea rather than on land, where the smugglers had it, more or less, all their own way. It was almost as if the golden age, exemplified so well by the passage which opens this book, had returned. The Battle of Trafalgar altered things on the smuggling front, however, just as it did to a far larger extent on the real fighting front, and many other places too, in the wars against the Corsican tyrant. For with the smashing of both the French and Spanish fleets came the release from service against the king's enemies without, and the return of the Revenue cutters back into service against the king's enemies within.

In 1806, the year following Trafalgar, most ports had a Revenue vessel on station, while at other places of less importance a guard patrolled in six-oared whalers. These vessels, to a greater or lesser extent, strove to work as well as they could with the poor old riding officers ashore. All this cooperation came not a minute too soon, for the damage the

Appearing in 1813, just two years before the Battle of Waterloo, this
cartoon is entitled 'Smuggling in High Life', and depicts a nobleman's
coach, with his lady on board, being searched by riding officers of the
Customs Service on the road from the port of Dover. The contraband
includes perfume, spirits, French cambric and even a document from
Napoleon himself (HM Customs & Excise)

smugglers were causing to the war effort once again had them very near
the top of the agenda for the hard-pressed government. That arch and
implacable enemy of the smugglers, Pitt, had died in 1806, and this must
have jerked those who were left into the realization that their efforts, re-
doubled, would have to fill the void, particularly in the war against the
smugglers. Nelson may have triumphed at the cost of his precious life,
but even he had not been able to do anything against the smugglers.

Such was the smugglers' growing insolence and profit, at the country's
expense, that in 1809 a completely new service was established, even
while the war was still going on with renewed vigour on land and sea:

the Preventive Waterguard, which was only made possible because of the lessening of the French and Spanish at sea to a negligible force and threat. The idea was that this new organization would be the vitally necessary link between the Revenue cruisers already noted on their stations round the coast, and the riding officers ashore. The measures even provided for these gentlemen to have their families compensated should they fall in the execution of their duty. Now the coast was divided into three districts, each under an inspecting commander. From Land's End to London forty-two preventive boats were supported by twenty-three cutters and sloops, and they had orders to attack any smuggling vessel which got past the larger vessels at sea. In bad weather the boats' crews went ashore and patrolled on foot, assisting the hard-pressed riding officers,* who must have wished that they had been dragoons rather than Jack Tars.

These sailors were always from faraway places, for it was government policy to post them where no family ties or obligations of friendship would compromise them in the execution of their one and only duty: the prevention of the running of contraband goods. It was never easy to find billets for these men in the environs of the small ports to which they were assigned, for in the staunch smuggling counties the local families, smugglers almost to a man, woman and child, refused to accept them into their homes, and the authorities were loath to make billeting compulsory. Therefore, living-quarters had to be added to the many watch-towers which were being hurriedly erected at smuggling trouble-spots. This meant that some period of hardship was inevitable, for while these buildings were going up on compulsorily purchased land, the sailors had to put up with living in tents which, though made of familiar canvas, must have been dreadful for them.[2]

These changes worked as well as could be expected in wartime, although they could hardly have been expected to make anything like the impression that was needed on the free trade. Nothing could really be done until Napoleon had been finally and incontrovertibly defeated, and when this happy event did suddenly happen, the changes on both

---

* The riding officers of Customs were, under these new arrangements, to be directed and inspected by newly appointed inspecting generals, a rank and post which had not existed before.

sides of the smuggling frontline were considerable. The first consequence was the release into the labour market of thousands of trained, seasoned and rather disgruntled seamen with no jobs. Of course, both the Board of Customs and the 'gentlemen of the night', as the smugglers liked to call themselves, were eager to employ these ex-servicemen, to say nothing of the thousands of trained soldiers who also came home. The government very sensibly increased the manning-levels of the Waterguard, taking the best men, for it was worried about the increase in the pre-war modes of smuggling which the peace would bring. In addition, the Admiralty took over the running of the Revenue cutters completely.

In 1816 the Treasury nervously warned of the destitute seamen who could not be absorbed by the Waterguard, and who 'will be the ready instruments of those desperate persons who have a little capital and are hardy enough to engage in the traffic of smuggling!'[3] For once a Treasury forecast was correct: smuggling was taking off in a big way and was now, in this post-war period, being practised by what seemed to be a new breed of smuggler, who had spent years at a time aboard rat-infested, floating hell-hulks which had been blockading half the world, with rarely a sight, let alone a feel, of any shore whether foreign or home, and under a form of discipline which no rabid dog would have been expected to endure. The hatred of these men for authority was far stronger than that felt by the smugglers of the pre-war period, even those who terrorized the county of Kent, and they had been trained to fight and to die in the finest school in the world: the Royal Navy. These men had been shown how to sail and shoot, board and repel boarders by officers, both warrant and commissioned, and now they wanted some of 'them wines and pickles' which those officers had always enjoyed (or so it was believed) in their own cabins and messes.

CHAPTER SEVEN

THE SCIENTIFIC AGE

The government's answer to the mushrooming problem of smuggling was to use a method of containment which had been supremely successful against the late enemy: blockade. However, instead of cutting Europe off from the rest of the world, it would cut Britain off from Europe, the difference being that the smugglers would be kept both in and out of the country at the same time. The other big decision was to give the cutter service over entirely to the Royal Navy. It was only natural to choose the coast of the two most troublesome counties along which to set up the blockade system. The idea had been the brainchild of a Captain Joseph McCulloch, RN, who had conceived it while on station in HMS *Ganymede* off the coast of Kent. He worked out and proposed the idea to the lords of the Admiralty, who in turn sent it along to the Treasury, which happily agreed to it as it promised to be a cost-effective effort to pen in the smugglers. By 1817 the coastal blockade was set up with Captain McCulloch as its commander. 'Flogging Joey', as he was known in the senior service, was the ideal man for the job for, as his nickname implied, he was a very strict officer and knew exactly what he was doing. He had seen the Waterguard in action and considered it little better than an undisciplined rabble. His own men, on the other hand, soon became known as 'The Warriors', for he trained them thoroughly in the use of their weapons, particularly the fearsome Royal Navy cutlass and the sea-musket.

Captain McCulloch's command was at first the coast between the North and South Forelands, and he used as his headquarters HMS *Ramillies*, anchored off Deal. Other relics of the late wars were pressed into service: the Martellos, those squat, menacing towers which never fired a shot in anger, for they had been built after Trafalgar, an engagement which had rendered them redundant as anti-invasion forts.

McCulloch was so successful with his coastal blockade system that it was extended from Sheerness to Beachy Head, and by 1824 every yard

The 'Warriors' was the name given to the men of the
Coast Blockade, the forerunner of the Coast Guard.
Here, two of them are practising their weapon skills

of that coastline was being watched and patrolled by 2,784 officers and
men. Chichester was the next extension limit, watch-houses and
Martellos having living-quarters added onto them. Each blockade station
had a detachment of men under a Royal Naval lieutenant. It was not
pleasant work: the men had to contend with bribery by the smugglers,
and if they did not play ball, or if they interrupted the running of

HMS *Ramillies* was the first headquarters of the Coastal Blockade Service, anchored in the Downs, off Deal in Kent

contraband, they tended to be hurled off the nearest steep cliff. Many of the Warriors died in small, pitched battles.

For those stretches of the smuggling coast not covered by the blockade a coast guard was provided in 1821, and it was, in fact, being discovered that the coastal blockade was not as effective as at first thought. Some authorities attributed this to Flogging Joey's strictness in enforcing

The Martello Tower was a great blessing to the 'Warriors', providing a
well-sited and strong station for them

In silent rowing boats the 'Warriors' patrolled not only the coast but also
the waters just off the shore, which surprised many a party of land-smugglers

discipline, and the danger, as well as the harsh living-conditions, for
recruitment of suitable types fell off, which could only have been
because of what they had heard of life in the new service. The truth was
that many of the men signing up for the coastal blockade were not up to
scratch, but the ranks had to be filled by men of some sort.[1]

The effect on personnel was one problem; the other was the effect on
the smugglers. They saw how very heavily armed the new enemy was,
and how resolute the best Warriors were to do their duty of

exterminating all smugglers, and so they responded in kind and, heavily armed, chose to carry on the war with authority in an even more formal military manner than ever before. So it was that the gentlemen of the night gradually resorted to the sort of violence that made the Hawkhurst Gang look like a cathedral choir on its best behaviour. They attacked the watch-houses and the Warriors' living-quarters in order to distract and pin them down when a run was being made. The smugglers even attacked some of the Martello towers, one raid in particular being in revenge for the patrol based there having captured four members of the attackers' gang, which was a fifty-strong outfit. Pitched battles became almost a matter of course: in some of the worst cases the heroic Warriors were attacked and then had to hold at bay hundreds of attacking smugglers while waiting desperately for reinforcements to come to their rescue. When such frightful struggles were over and charges had been brought, the local courts were even less helpful than they had been before the French Wars broke out, acquitting palpably guilty smugglers by the dozen.

Once again it was the Treasury and not the Admiralty or the Board of Customs, which, worried by the rocketing cost of containing the outlaws and the sneaking suspicion that the blockade system was not really delivering, decided that what was desperately needed was an overall controlling director, so that the various elements of the preventive service could really deal a knockout blow to the smugglers. So it was that the Treasury recommended most strongly that the Waterguard, as well as the cutter force, should go back under the control of the Board of Customs; that the riding officers should be reduced to a force only fifty strong; and that the larger preventive cruisers should remain firmly under Admiralty control. Then on 15 January 1822 it was announced that the coastal blockade and the other preventive services would be combined and called 'the Coast Guard'. A new commander was appointed: Captain William Bowles of the Royal Navy, whose title and rank was to be Comptroller General. He would be responsible directly to the Board of Customs, for the sole concern of his new force was the 'protection of the Revenue'. His officers were to be nominated by the Admiralty, all RN men, for the Coast Guard was to have everything naval style: there would never again be any shilly-shallying between riding officers and dragoons, for instance, because of the Revenue men being neither Army nor Navy, and therefore despised by both. The Coast Guard was to be the Royal Navy's first reserve, which meant that its men would be called up for active service before all others whenever national need demanded, and the Navy would get experienced, trained men through the active service which would be the everyday lot of all Coast Guards in their continuous war against the smugglers.[2]

The new service was left in no doubt that its prime duty was to get the smugglers and put them where they would never defraud His Majesty of his Customs again. They were to be fought with the heaviest weapons and a military force, operating on both sea and land, which was supplied, organized and directed with full military precision. It was Captain Bowles's first job to lay down what he expected of his men, and this he did in his 'General Instructions':

Article 1. General Instructions for the Coast Guard of the United Kingdom: 1829.

Issued by Captain William Bowles, R.N., Comptroller General of the Revenue Coast Guard in the United Kingdom of Great Britain and Ireland.

To the respective Inspectors General, Inspecting Commanders, Commanders, Officers and Crews of Cruisers, Chief Officers and Crews of Stations, and the Mounted Guard.

GENERAL INSTRUCTIONS All Officers and Persons employed in the Coast Guard are to bear in mind that the sole object of their appointment is the protection of the Revenue, and that their utmost endeavours are therefore to be used to prevent the landing of uncustomed goods, and to seize all persons, vessels, boats, cattle and carriages in any way employed in smuggling, and all goods liable to be forfeited by law.

Every Person in the Coast Guard is to consider it his first and most important object to secure the person of the Smuggler; and the reward granted for each Smuggler convicted, or share of the penalty recovered from him, will be paid, on the certificate of the Inspecting Commander to the person or persons by whom the Smuggler is absolutely taken and secured, and not to the crew in general.

Every Officer and Person employed in the Coast Guard is hereby strictly charged not to do, consent to, abet or conceal any act or thing wherein or whereby His Majesty's Revenue may be injured or defrauded, but to use his utmost endeavours for its protection, and to prevent all frauds and abuses therein, the Officers holding Deputations always remembering the Solemn Oath taken at their admission: that they will truly and faithfully execute the Trust committed to their charge, according to the best of their knowledge and power.

Every Officer and other Person employed in the Coast Guard is strictly enjoined to a cordial and active co-operation with the different branches of the Service, as well as with every other description of force employed for the protection and security of the Revenue, and no offence will be more severely punished than any failure in this respect by which the Revenue may receive injury, either from the negligence, want of cordiality, or self-interested feelings of any individual. [There follow paragraphs emphasizing the need for constant communication between Coast Guard officers and the Customs officers within ports, for accurate statements and reports by all coast guards, and for all guardsmen to know the anti-smuggling laws and these Coast Guard instructions very well indeed.]

Every Officer and Person employed in the Coast Guard is to take special care that at all times the Service is conducted with as little expense to the Revenue as is practicable, consistent with its security.

The whole of the Officers and Persons employed in the Coast Guard are clearly to understand that the property of the Crown is in no way, either directly or indirectly, to be made the source of private emolument, and any deviation from this principle will be considered as a most serious offence.

Writs of Assistance are essential for searching buildings for contraband; and a report on each search is to be made to the Comptroller General for the information of the Board.

It is the duty of the Coast Guard to search and strictly examine all suspicious ships, vessels and boats coming within the limits of their Stations, respectively, and to seize all goods prohibited to be imported or exported, and other goods liable to forfeiture found on board, together with the ship, vessel and boats (if liable to seizure), and also to detain the masters and crews, where the law authorises such a proceeding.

The Coast Guards are to watch all outward bound vessels having Drawback, Bounty or Prohibited Goods on board, or goods taken out of bonded warehouses, in order to prevent the relanding thereof within the limits of their respective Stations. If any part of a cargo is illegally unshipped they are to seize the same, together with the boat in which it is found, and also the vessel, (where liable under any act for the prevention of Smuggling), if practicable, making an immediate report of the particulars to the Investigating Commander and the principal Officers of the Customs at the nearest Port.

All Officers are to be on their guard against a common practice among vessels returning from a voyage with coals, etc., to any foreign port, of putting contraband goods on their return into light vessels from London or on the coast, but chiefly to cobles or fishing-boats at sea; and great care is to be observed in searching such vessels when met within the distance prescribed by Law, whether they be fishing-vessels, vessels coming from the coast, or otherwise. It being also a common practice for colliers proceeding to and from the west coast of England, etc., to call at some port on the Continent for contraband goods, which they conceal in their cargoes or ballast, great care is to be observed in examining all such vessels, and every opportunity is to be taken to obtain information from time to time at the Custom Houses of what vessels are cleared outward for ports on the Continent, and when they may be expected back, and also to obtain a description of such vessels in order to the better discovering them on their return.

Whenever a vessel is met with that is bound to a British port, and the Commander or Chief Officer . . . shall, after searching her, have reason to believe that . . . Goods liable to duty may still be concealed on board for the purpose of being clandestinely landed before the vessel arrives at her port of discharge, he is to place on board such vessel an Officer and one or more trusty persons, with instructions to keep a strict and constant watch to prevent any such goods from being so landed, and to deliver the said vessel and cargo into the charge of the proper officers at the port to which she is bound, informing them if he shall have discovered during his stay on board any further suspicious circumstances relative to the vessel or cargo, and directing him when he shall have completed the service on which he has been employed, to return the man to his vessel or Station, as the case may be. The Commander or Chief Officer is also to transmit by the person he may send in charge of such vessel a letter to the Collector and

Comptroller of the port stating the cause of his being so sent. All the proceedings herein are to be reported to the Inspecting Commander.

When any vessel is met with by a cruiser or the boat of a station which, upon enquiry and observation, there shall be just cause to suspect of having any articles on board intended to be smuggled or privately landed: if seen by a cruiser, she is diligently to watch such vessel, and keep her company 'till she be seen clear of the coast, or until the observation of her can be transferred to a neighbouring cruiser . . . and if by the boat of a Station, she is to be watched as far as possible, or until the suspicions can be communicated to a cruiser, as circumstances will permit; and if any vessel wholly or in part laden as aforesaid, shall voluntarily come into any port, harbour, bay, creek or other place . . . and delay to prosecute her voyage with the first opportunity of wind and weather without just cause, the commander of any cruiser, or Chief Officer of a Station, who may detect such proceeding, is to detain such vessel, (if liable), and lading [cargo], and deliver the same to the Collector and Comptroller of the nearest port, with proof of her voluntarily coming in, and transmit information of the same to the Inspecting Commander for further directions. A more special regard is to be had herein to such small vessels whose construction, etc., bespeak them as fit for the purposes of smuggling, and not for foreign trade, in which they often pretend to be employed.

When a smuggling vessel is chased and the goods are thrown overboard, the chase is not to be given up to take possession of such goods, but the pursuit continued whilst there is any probability of coming up with, and securing, the vessel and crew; and in order that all chance of recovering the goods may not be lost, a mark buoy is to be thrown overboard at such time as may appear most likely to lead to their discovery.

When any ship or vessel is seized or detained, the hatches are to be sealed up, and every possible care taken that she may be delivered to the Collector or Comptroller without any manner of embezzlement.

Vessels' manifests are to be required from their masters and copies are to be sent to the Officers of Customs and other interested parties.

Any incautious or wanton use of firearms on the part of Officers or persons employed in the Coast Guard will be visited with the severest displeasure of the Board.

Before firing to bring to any vessel or boat liable to seizure or examination under any Act or Law for the prevention of Smuggling, whether by night or day, the proper ensign or pendant are always to be displayed on board cruisers and boats. And it is particularly to be observed that no Officer commanding any cruiser or boat can be justified in firing at, or into, any ship or vessel that does not bring to on being required to do so, or on being chased for that purpose, unless the said colours shall be hoisted, and a gun or musquet fired as a signal. . . . And if any person shall be killed or wounded by any shot fired before these requisites have been performed, the person or persons by whom and by whose order such shot is fired, must abide the due course of law, the Officers observing that no vessel can be fired at except such as are liable to seizure and examination under some law for the prevention of Smuggling.

Before candles are used in the examination of vessels, the greatest care is to be taken, in order to avoid accidents by Fire, that they are properly secured in sound Lanterns.

The Officers of the Coast Guard are to endeavour to obtain information respecting smuggling on every description, and to communicate the same, with any other intelligence likely to benefit the Revenue, as opportunities occur, to the Inspecting Commanders, Commanders of Cruisers, Chief Officers of Stations, Officers of Customs or Excise, and any other person or persons in the neighbourhood employed for the protection of the Revenue; and also to take every opportunity of communicating with each other for the purpose of obtaining intelligence.

Inspecting Commanders and all other Officers and persons are to be extremely cautious how they give credit to, or act on, information coming from a source with which they are not well acquainted: false information being very frequently offered.

All information has to be reported to the Inspecting Commander, and no agreement to pay for it must be entered into.

If, notwithstanding the utmost vigilance and exertion of the Coast Guard to detect the running of Contraband Goods, it shall at any time happen that a quantity shall be smuggled at any place within their respective Stations, the Commanders of cruisers and Chief Officers are not only to exert themselves to the utmost to discover and seize the said goods on shore, but more especially to use their best endeavours to find out the fishing or other boat or boats that were employed in receiving or landing the same, and to seize them, provided there is sufficient proof of their having been so employed. They will likewise endeavour to discover the names of their owners, and of the persons who were actually employed in navigating them, and in unshipping and receiving the said goods; also the names and places of residence of such persons as may be brought forward as witnesses to prove their being so employed and concerned.

The most particular attention is to be paid to any signals which may from time to time be established for the purpose of communicating intelligence between the different cruisers and stations.

The Officers and crews of the Coast Guard are to be civil and obliging to the inhabitants, never to interfere with them and their concerns, unless when necessary for the due execution of their duty; and in those cases to be particularly careful that no just cause of complaint be given. They are strictly enjoined not to destroy Game, encroach on Manors, or interfere with Manorial or other Rights; to avoid trespassing on Private Property as much as possible, and when they may have occasion to pass over private grounds, or cultivated lands in the execution of their duty, they are to be extremely careful not to damage the same, and to pass and re-pass by the gates and other entrances when practicable. They are to be respectful and obedient to the local Magistrates and authorities.

No boat is to be sent on duty without the Deputed Officer.

The Arms are always to be kept clean: wallpieces, musquets and pistols properly flinted, ammunition dry, and the whole in every respect fit for service; and when persons return from duty the greatest care is to be taken that their arms are lodged in places of security, and each individual is held responsible for this duty.

Cruisers and boats are only to be employed for the service and carry no passengers and not to be used for pleasure-cruises.

No Officer or Man serving in the Coast Guard is allowed to possess any business, or the share of any business, public-house or shop, or directly or indirectly, either in his own name or in the name of any other person or persons whomsoever, or in company or partnership with any others, to trade as a merchant, or factor, or agent, for any

This Midshipman is hardly a youth, but he was thankful to find
employment in the 'Warriors' after the contraction of the Royal Navy in
1815. He would be second-in-command of a Coastal Blockade station
under a Royal Naval Lieutenant

others, in any goods, wares or merchandise, or have any occupation or
employment whatever other than his situation in the Coast Guard.

Commanding Officers are on no account to go out on duty
without their commissions about their persons.

Commissions are to be taken up as soon as possible after
appointment.

Any person wishing to quit the Service must deliver to his Commanding Officer a written notice of his intention twenty-eight days prior to the day on which he wishes to be discharged, in order that the same may be forwarded to the Inspecting Commander for the sanction of the Comptroller General.

No Officer or other persons employed in the Coast Guard is to crave any travelling allowance or subsistence in consequence of his having been engaged in the pursuit of goods run or intended to be run, or in looking out in expectation of making seizures, the law having in such cases given to the seizing Officer a share of the penalties and forfeitures as an encouragement and recompense for that service.

Certificates of baptism are required from all persons on their admission to the Coast Guard service, excepting Officers of the Navy. . . . No person, excepting Officers in the Royal Navy, is to be admitted into the Service in any capacity if he exceeds the age of thirty years, and is under twenty.

The Crown is not liable to the payment of the funeral expenses of Officers or Men belonging to the Coast Guard, but the Board will not object to the application of any monies which may be due to parties dying in the Service, in liquidation of such charges.

As complaints against Officers and Men belonging to the Coast Guard for non-payment of debts are highly discreditable to the Service, they are strictly enjoined to pay all just demands on them punctually and honestly. And they are to observe that no person will be promoted or receive any mark of favour or confidence against whom complaints of this description are on record.[3]

There are thirty-one further articles in the 'General Instructions', and they lay down the most detailed procedures for every eventuality which a coast guard, be he man or officer, could possibly come upon in the pursuit of his duty. The order of command throughout the service is laid out: the role of the inspecting commanders, the commanders of the coast guard ships on constant patrol at sea, the cruisers, the chief officers, the crews of the cruisers, and the crews of the shore-based stations, which were run like the 'stone frigates' of the Royal Navy. The Mounted Guard had their own instructions set out in the eighth article: they had formerly been the riding officers of Customs, and they were still using the handbook written for their guidance as long ago as 1734. Another article dealt with district carpenters, another with extra men; while article XI directed that: '. . . smugglers to serve in the Royal Navy are to be conveyed to Guard Ships in close custody whilst on board Coast Guard Cruisers . . . Returns of smugglers must be made; descriptions of smugglers who escape must be given; and subsistence for smugglers in custody ashore is to be drawn at 2/6d per day.' Seizures and boats were dealt with in articles XII and XIII, while the next gave an interesting insight into stores in general and in particular 'One set of rummaging tools: one gravel spit, six gimlets, two tucks, three hammers, one tomahawk, one crow, two shovels, and one dark lantern'.

Buildings, cruisers, pay and allowances, superannuation, pensions and gratuities to widows and children of coast guards killed in combat with the smugglers, dying as a result of wounds and injuries, or death by drowning, by accident or as a result of injuries received in accidents were all dealt with, as well as courts of inquiry and investigations. Being dismissed from the service was the penalty for 'any person conniving, or being intimate with smugglers, or making any engagement with them, or neglecting to apprehend them, or suffering them to escape after apprehension, or guilty of wilful negligence, want of courage or exertion by which persons or goods escape capture, or any speculation, embezzlement, or of making any false musters, or of injuring the property of the Crown, either directly or indirectly', after a court of inquiry had established guilt.

The last few articles covered provisions for leave of absence, letters, and keeping of full and accurate journals (such a marked feature of the old-style riding officers' duties), the wearing and care of uniforms, pilotage of vessels by coast guards, victualling of both ships and shore stations, how to deal with cases needing quarantine, the treatment of pensioners in hospitals, and the complicated procedures necessary in cases of shipwreck. It is the penultimate article which deals with 'Apparatus for Saving Lives'. The coast guards' 'most important object' may have been to secure the person of the smuggler, but in the end he was expected to save the lives of mariners in danger as well, two priorities which have, in fact, been reversed over the years. Rescuing seamen and passengers from beached vessels, or those being ground to pieces on rocks during storms was exceedingly difficult; it was not until

Lord Nelson's friend George Manby perfected his mortar which could fire 500 yd of line from shore to ship that rescue could be carried out effectively. This mortar and the coast guards' other life-saving equipment was fully dealt with in this article.

The most important piece of equipment for the new force, however, was undoubtedly the new watch-house building, which was erected wherever smuggling was known to be rife. In some cases it replaced the long-established preventive station, but there were far more of them, for beats had to be established which the coast guards would patrol twenty-four hours a day. In the report of the committee set up by the Treasury in 1821, which examined in great detail the several services fighting the smugglers, and from which the formation of the Coast Guard sprang, a new attitude to smuggling was clearly expressed in the final paragraph. There were to be no more half-measures – a military answer was the only solution to the festering problem of smuggling:

> We think, indeed, that from the moment when a disposition has been manifested by the body of smugglers to offer an organised and armed resistance to the military and civil functions of the public, the force directed against them should be such as to leave them neither chance nor hopes of success. Every principle of policy and every consideration of humanity forbid that the means employed against those deluded persons should be either really or apparently so nearly balanced with their own strength as to give any degree of encouragement to men stimulated as they are by the prospect of great gain to undertake, or to protract, so pernicious a contest.

So the trained men of the Coast Guard, strong and resolute, were out in all weathers, patrolling the coasts with military precision and regularity, in foul weather stoutly clothed in great-coats and suits of oilskin, and, in particularly bitter weather, in sheepskin jackets too. They were heavily armed, with greater fire-power at their disposal than the average soldier of the period: they carried musket and bayonet, the heavy naval cutlass, a brace of pistols, and to help them see and signal they had telescopes and lamps. In addition, with typical Royal Navy forethought, they were issued with stools on which they could sit on their cliff-edges and keep watch. However, these 'one-legged donkeys', as they called them, were

A coast guard on watch in summer uniform

no ordinary stools: they could perch on them but they could not sleep on them.

The Coast Guard stations were remarkably commodious: each had an officer's house for the commander of the station, always a lieutenant, many of them had five bedrooms, two sitting-rooms, a kitchen, a scullery and a pantry. There could be anything up to ten Coast Guard

The Coast Guard station, a typical 'stone frigate', with flagpole flying the
Union flag and official pennant. The stations were carefully sited for
maximum surveillance in smuggling trouble-spots, and were run with
military precision and discipline

cottages, each often having three bedrooms, a living-room and the usual
offices; and there was usually the boathouse attached to the store, the
office, chart-room and the watch-house or room, the heart of the
station. Naval discipline was the order of the day, the commanding
officer inspecting all parts of his establishment to see that it was clean,
tidy and efficient.

The 'General Instructions' extended to the coast guard's family life:
'No individual can be appointed to any Station within twenty miles of
the place of his birth, or within twenty miles of the place at which he
has resided for the six months previous to his appointment.' And coast
guards could not marry whomsoever they chose: 'Any man inter-
marrying with the family of a reputed or notorious smuggler, or lodging
in his house, or contracting an improper intimacy with him, will be
dismissed.' In the stations, wives who could not get on with their
neighbours in the other cottages and quarrelled interminably were to be
transferred with their husbands elsewhere, their menfolk bearing the
expense of the move. And the loyal wives could not have been too
happy about the long hours the men were made to work, for shifts of
anything up to fifteen hours were not uncommon when the smugglers
were being particularly troublesome.

The watch-house of the Coast Guard station which was built on the shore
at Lepe, Hampshire, to control the entrance to the Beaulieu river, a
favourite smugglers' highway

To ensure that information was not being passed on to the smugglers,
the guards were not told the beats they were to patrol on a given night
until immediately before they went out of the station to do their duty.
There seems to have been little trust on the part of the officers: a strict
system of fines dealt with breaches of the rules, with dismissal from the
service, as we have seen, as the final sanction. In a time of few jobs and
substandard housing for the lower orders, to be ejected from the steady
work, regular pay and, above all, excellent housing was a fate to be
feared by all coast guards. The comptroller general made it clear to all his

PARDON.

WHEREAS it has been humbly represented to the KING, that divers large bodies of Armed Smugglers have lately been feloniously assembled on different parts of the Coasts of Kent and Sussex, for the purpose of effecting the Landing of Uncustomed and Prohibited Goods;— And Whereas, upon such occasions, violent attacks have been made upon the Officers and Men in His Majesty's Coast Guard Service, and upon the Officers of Customs, in which several Persons have been Killed and severely Wounded;—And Whereas it is necessary to put an end to such Outrages and to bring the Offenders to Justice;—HIS MAJESTY, for the better discovering the Persons who have been guilty of these Felonies and Murders, is hereby pleased to promise His Most Gracious

PARDON

to any one or more of the Persons so assembled, (except those who actually committed violence upon the said Officers and Men) who shall discover his Accomplices, so that they may be apprehended and brought to Justice.   MELBOURNE.

And the Commissioners of His Majesty's Customs are hereby pleased to offer the following

REWARDS

for the Detection and Apprehension of Persons who have been concerned in such Offences, that is to say,

£1000

to any Person or Persons who shall discover or cause to be discovered any Person or Persons by whose agreement or undertaking such companies were so illegally assembled, or the actual Perpetrator or Perpetrators of any such Murders.

£500

to any Person or Persons who shall discover or cause to be discovered any Person or Persons who was or were Armed with Fire Arms or other Offensive Weapons, and assembled to the number of Three or more for the purpose of running such Uncustomed and Prohibited Goods, and

£200

to any Person or Persons who shall discover or cause to be discovered any one or more of such Offenders who were concerned in the running of such Goods. The above Rewards to be paid by the Collector and Comptroller of Customs at the Port of Rye upon the conviction of any such Offenders.

Custom House, London,
2d March, 1832.   THOS. WHITMORE, Sec.

[By Authority:—J. Hartnell, Fleet Street, London.]

A Board of Customs poster for Kent and Sussex from 1832. The government was optimistic about the way the war was going against the smugglers, who were now feeling the strength of the Coast Guard subordinates that strict records were being kept of all successful smuggling runs and that both officers and men in the areas of stations where these happened would automatically have fewer chances of promotion than those coast guards in areas where the smugglers were totally prevented, through their efforts, from plying their forbidden trade. Nor could men unsuccessful in their duties expect consideration in matters such as compassionate pleas, for the new service was completely unforgiving.

They were encouraged to be merciless to the smugglers: it was a coast guard who was the first Englishman to use the terrible weapon of swanshot against his compatriots, when he fired on smugglers. From this incident came the order to all coast guards to cut their ball bullets into four segments so that their fire would, it was hoped, be four times more effective when they had to shoot down smugglers. The policy was to attack first, before the smugglers could summon assistance, for they would obviously bring hundreds of helpers from the surrounding seaside if the need arose. Coast guards were enjoined never to fire into the air to summon assistance if they were beset by the enemy, so that not a single shot would be wasted. A runner had to be sent to summon help. This obsession with attacking and arresting the smugglers was drummed into the men, and the goods being smuggled were regarded as of little consequence, a set of priorities reflected in the system of rewards, for the coast guards were given no prize-money for the goods they seized but only for the smugglers they apprehended.

The 'General Instructions' laid great emphasis on the gathering of intelligence, and money was allowed for the bribing of local people round the stations to give information about intended runs of contraband and the other doings of the enemy. However, it was not an easy way of gaining knowledge, for the coast guards were forbidden to mix with the locals socially, and were confined to their station quarters when not on patrol on their beats. The smugglers, on the other hand, found, as they always had, that intelligence of their enemies' movements was easy to come by, and few bribes were needed. Where leaks of information were discovered and names were forthcoming, instant dismissal from the service was the inevitable result.

The fortitude of these early coast guards was amazing. Ruled with a rod of iron both on- and off-duty, their professional lives were full of hard work, little reward and the constant possibility of wounding and violent death. They were at their busiest in the very depths of winter and at night, for these were the smugglers' favoured seasons and hours, as they always had been. Fog, sea-mist, low cloud, gales and storms, freezing cold together with the constant roar of heavy seas breaking on rough coasts were the allies of the smugglers, just as they were the tormentors and enemies of the poor benighted coast guards. They trudged through their patrols and kept their freezing vigils, and when action faced them, as it did suddenly and usually without warning, they almost invariably went into battle with enthusiasm. In many a churchyard in the maritime counties of this country there can be found headstones placed there to the memory of coast guards who died as a result of being ordered into action against massed smugglers, or because they surprised the enemy when on their relentless patrols. In the graveyard at Kimmeridge, Dorset, near Clavel's Tower, already mentioned on p. 61, the fates of coast guards are recorded, such as one who was 'killed by his own firearms in the execution of his duty'; a second who was 'drowned in the Bay at night in the execution of his duty'; and a third who 'lost his life by accidentally falling over the cliff while in the execution of his duty'. Not all deaths were results of direct action by the smugglers, which must have made them all the harder to bear for the grieving loved ones.

Once the Coast Guard stations had been set up in every possible smuggling location, the grip of the new service closed on the smugglers and made sure that not one of them was unaffected by it. In the ports they also became a real thorn in the side of the crews of ships who were in the habit of carrying contraband hidden in and beneath legitimate goods. The result was that the smuggling sailors had to find more and more ingenious ways of concealing their smuggled goods than ever before. The scientific age had well and truly arrived.

Contraband was often transhipped halfway across the Channel, or the North Sea, a process which went by the strange name of 'coopering', from French, Dutch or Scandinavian vessels into British coasters; the smugglers would have the remainder of their voyages to stow the contraband goods securely behind false bulkheads; between decks and keel; behind panelling and outer skin in cabins; in hollow spars or spare masts; in oars which had been carefully hollowed out; and inside coils of

The cooper worked almost exclusively among the
fishermen of the Dogger Bank, off the coast of Yorkshire
in the North Sea. Working out of one of the European
ports, he carried mainly tobacco and spirits which he sold
to the hardy fishermen, taking fish or goods in payment,
both of which were the property of the fishing-boat's
owner, and not the fishermen

Once the coast guards had realized that most suspicious ships had false
bulkheads, the smugglers had to devise even subtler hiding-places. The
sectioning of a ship's water-cask became a favourite. Constructing such
ingenious barrels demanded exceptional coopering skills

rope. The smugglers of tobacco even perfected the art of making a skein
of real tobacco look like a length of rope neatly coiled up on the deck.
Every barrel, whatever its size, was suspected by the Coast Guard
'gaugers', as their rummage-crew members were called; the obliging
coopers who plied their craft specifically for the smugglers had been
making barrels with false sides, bottoms, lids and every other possible
component, so that when the gauger inserted his dipstick, it came out
with water on it if it was a water-cask, and not with the brandy which
was stored in the secret section. Bales of textiles were ideal for
concealing all kinds of smaller items; food not consumed during the
course of a voyage would be brought ashore, apparently for use in the
sailors' homes, but in actual fact concealing silk kerchiefs, gloves and
similar high-value items of contraband. Geese and turkeys were
favourites for this sort of work, but even the humble loaf of bread was
used.

As had always been the case, brandy and gin remained so highly
profitable that even small amounts preserved from the prying eyes, noses
and poking-sticks of the Coast Guard rummagers and gaugers were
worth smuggling. One of the most effective ways of getting the liquor
ashore from the coasting ships was to use the 'belly canteen'. Made of

the thinnest sheet-iron so that it resembled a rather large stomach, it could hold up to two gallons. It most probably originated in Scotland where belly canteens were regularly used by the whisky smugglers, usually women, who ran much of the illicit traffic across the border between Scotland, where the whisky distilleries were, and England. Most of that traffic seems to have finished up in the city of Carlisle.

It was ingenious inventions such as these that had turned smuggling into the science it had had to become, simply because of the effectiveness of the Coast Guard. Another scientific invention was the smuggling 'torpedo'. Made of canvas in the shape of a very large and long sausage, it was packed with contraband along a rigid frame, padded, and a waterproof outer casing stitched over it. It was weighted to make it float just below the surface behind a vessel coming into a port, and was towed on a line which could be easily slipped if the Coast Guard took undue interest in what was going on. This streamlined smuggling container prefigured the famous 'Whisky torpedo', so popular with the bootleggers-at-sea of the Prohibition period in 1920s America.

The greatest innovation of this scientific age was the development and refinement of the device used in the earlier golden age, known as 'rafting'. This method of getting spirit-kegs ashore used, in its simplest form, a pole with the barrels lashed loosely along its length, and with weights at intervals, so arranged that the raft floated just above the sea-bed. Allowed to go up an inlet or harbour on the flood-tide, the raft would ground in the shallows where watchers would be waiting to receive it and get it ashore. This rafting technique was used in estuaries, usually harbours, with their multifarious in-coming streams, both great and small, running down to the main sheet of water. The whole area was affected by the tides which enabled the smugglers, who knew such matters intimately, to float their goods in through the harbour entrances, which were usually very narrow, right under the very noses of their sworn enemies the coast guards, whose watch-houses overlooked these entrances for the precise purpose of preventing smuggling. But the Coast Guard had not yet caught up with submarine smuggling, and it was this that the smugglers were making the most of. It was Captain Frederick Marryat who, after considerable experience at sea of the smugglers and their methods, wrote to the Admiralty in 1822 and revealed the full cunning of the contraband-running inventors who were to make this

The original 'bootlegger'. Any tobacco or cigars left in
the fishing-boats served by the 'coopers' when they came
into port was smuggled ashore under the noses of the
Customs officers in the fishermen's sea-boots. This was
known as 'bootlegging'

phase of smuggling so difficult for the government and its preventive services.

Another method involved securing a 200 fathom line of strong twine to a secure post at the upper limit of the harbour, and then taking the reel out to sea in a lobster or crab-fishing boat, playing out the line as it went down the harbour and out through its entrance, past the watching coast guards. Once out of sight of the watchers, well out to sea, the end of the line would be secured by a diver to the waiting submerged raft of kegs, and then, as the flood-tide swelled and streamed into the harbour, it would be drawn inwards past the ubiquitous guards.

In harbours like those of Portsmouth and neighbouring Langstone, the Coast Guard always closed off the mouth by mounting a standing, or rather a rowing guard, constantly patrolling backwards and forwards across the harbour mouths. In such places the smugglers had to make sure that they could get their rafts under the guard-boats, and for this purpose they made use of the services of men like Abe Coakes, the swimming smuggler of Mudeford. The smuggling vessel would approach the mouth of the harbour with about thirty tubs of spirits slung like a great necklace round the gunwales and hanging over the sides. When the captain decided his ship had arrived at the right spot offshore, the 'stops' along the tops of the gunwales would be cut away smartly, or released by pulling slip-knots, and the necklace would drop into the water, the flooding tide taking it towards the mouth of the harbour. If a sailor was slow with releasing one of the stops while the others were undone, the ship stood a very good chance of being capsized by its own illicit cargo. An improvement was eventually made when the smugglers found how to hold the running-line with the tubs attached by another single line running round the tops of the gunwales and which could be released by undoing a single knot on the captain's word of command. This system seemed to be a more reliable one.

Abe Coakes would be in the water awaiting the smuggler, and directly the raft was in the water and starting to move with the current he began his skilled task of marshalling, towing and tweaking the great, ungainly conglomeration of ropes, tubs and weights towards the harbour mouth through which the incoming tide was urging it. Coakes had to ensure that nothing snagged and, particularly, that no part grounded on the floor of the harbour, for the sand bars are still, to this day, notoriously liable to shifting and changing their shape and even location. He would have to keep the submerged raft in the main channel, which he would have had to check before the run to see what changes had been wrought in it by the action of the waters of the two mighty rivers, the Avon and Stour, which unite above Christchurch Harbour proper. Abe Coakes is locally credited with being able to get his rafts far beyond the head of the harbour into either of the rivers, for several miles as far as the tide reaches. It must have been dangerous, cold and laborious work for the swimming smuggler of Mudeford; but he went on doing it for many years, fooling the coast guards year in and year out until someone decided to try and claim the £500 reward still available to anyone lodging information leading to the arrest and conviction of a smuggler. Someone informed on Abe Coakes and he was caught: his swimming and rafting days were over.[4]

In the larger harbours with much wider mouths the incoming smuggling vessels attached a light-buoy to float just above the half-sunken raft as it was taken up through the harbour or river by the inflowing tide. This light-buoy had a lantern divided into two sections, one above the other. The top section had no window, the candle only showing its light when it burned down below the 'floor' between the upper and lower sections. This, of course, only happened when the raft was way up the inlet and out of danger of being spotted by the Coast Guard. Those who would see it were the ever-vigilant watchers of the shallows.

One of the greatest features of the rafting system was the fact that even if a raft *was* discovered by the Coast Guard they had no proof of who it belonged to, from which ship it had been launched, nor, indeed, who had shepherded it through the watery mazes of its strange voyage.

However, the Coast Guard gradually became better and better at surprising the smugglers into abandoning many of their rafts, and they improved their techniques for finding 'crops', or loads of tubs, which had been sunk for the purpose of being collected later. Where they suspected a crop to have been dumped, they would send two boats, rowing parallel, to creep up on the contraband. At first they used weighted anchors, which were dragged along the bottom in the hope that their flukes would catch one of the ropes linking the kegs and weights together. As the guards gained more experience and

The 'creepers' were used by the Coast Guard to find 'the crop' before the
smugglers did, and so claim their prize-money. They made full use of their
oared boats just as their forerunners in the Coastal Blockade had done

demanded more efficiency in these methods, they realized that special
designs were essential if they were to gain any measurable success. So
the grapnels and 'creepers' were developed, as well as the more
complex 'centipedes'.

As was always the case, as their opposition got more crafty and
successful at recovering contraband goods, so the smugglers evolved the
necessary counter-measures. They took to sinking their crops not on
flat, sandy sea-beds, but among submarine rocks, in huge beds of
seaweed, or among masses of crab and lobster-pots. Here, in these places,
the smugglers hoped the coast guards' grapnels of various kinds would
be snagged and never even touch their kegs and ropes; but the guards
designed a special instrument for just such difficulties and it worked with
considerable success.

These crops had, of course, to be marked, and this was done either
by taking bearings on seamarks on the shore, for example church spires,
white buildings such as farmhouses, or headlands. The smugglers also
used cork floats, which were so weighted that they rode just below the
surface, the only indication of their position being a feather. When the
coast was clear of their enemies, the coast guards, the smugglers would
row out in the same manner as their foe but with a far better idea of
where they had to search for their waiting crop. The free traders even
had a special term for brandy or gin which had been left a little too

long under the water and had gone off: 'stinkibus'. Should the Coast
Guard enquire as to their intended business out at sea as they passed the
harbour bar, the smugglers would simply say that they had lobster or
crab-pots to attend to and that they would be back quite soon, omitting
to mention what they hoped to be carrying deep in the hold as their
main cargo, for the kegs would be carefully covered by lobsters, crabs or
even seaweed, the usual bed for such creatures. Very often on a fishing
voyage during which contraband had been acquired from whatever
source, a covering of bona fide fish was laid over the illicit goods, and
the ship took its time returning to its home port so that the fish would
acquire a rather rich aroma, one calculated to discourage even the most
officious rummager from searching the incoming vessel. Such sailors'
tricks must have been very confusing and frustrating for coast guards
unused to the ways of the sea in general and fishermen in particular,
especially when they were smugglers.

However, the guards were determined to learn, and whenever they
discovered a previously unknown smugglers' dodge, they noted every
detail of it down and had the description printed off and circulated to
every Coast Guard watch-house in the country. In this way, the whole
service was kept up to date on whatever the smugglers might do to fool
them. For the smugglers it meant yet more planning and experiments to
develop yet more ingenious methods, and all this left less time to run
goods.

Some smuggling vessels were so drastically redesigned that they had
false keels which could be filled with contraband. When the
determined spot had been reached these keels could be released to sink
to the bottom of the sea. Above deck several smuggling vessels found it
convenient to have a change of sails, both in colour and combination
of shapes, so that they could alter them to avoid identification by the
Coast Guard ships at sea. Others added a false mast, which wasn't used
for hoisting sails but which became, in fact, a long, thin vertical
container for contraband, with plugs for loading which would be
painted over and varnished every time the mast was filled with
whatever was being smuggled. Even merchant ships, which carried
mainly legal cargo that the crews were quite happy for the gaugers to
check, usually had a number of false bulkheads and an assortment of
secret hides in the panelling.[5]

Of course, there were many one-off dodges which the quick-witted habitual smugglers seized upon for their use when the opportunity arose. One smuggling ship was wrecked on the coast of Holland and several of the crew were presumed to have drowned. The captain had the bodies shipped back to his home port in coffins and supervised their loading into horse-drawn hearses on the quayside under the gaze of both grieving relatives and the ever-present coast guards, who paid the proper respects to their deceased enemies. The cortège called at each cottage where a coffin was dropped off, and it was only when a coast guard called on one of these to show his concern that the trick was discovered. He found the family of the deceased, smugglers all, gloating over the open coffin which contained, not a corpse, but a vast amount of contraband of various sorts.

Another funeral run of a similar nature involved the coffin of a woman who had, it was put about, died in France. The most elaborate arrangements were made in the port of Dover to receive her casket, which, of course, was empty of any body but full of the finest Chantilly and Valenciennes lace.

The increasing control over the smugglers on land was matched by the growing numbers and efficiency of the anti-smuggling ships at sea which assisted the Coast Guard. Almost every captain was a Royal Navy lieutenant, and the vessels themselves could be anything up to 140 tons. Launched in 1834, while steam was still in its infancy at sea, the steam-powered *Vulcan* was the greatest innovation. Her commissioning certainly showed how much in the forefront the Coast Guard was in everything which would advance the greater efficiency of the service.

This inexorable process of growing strength in the 1830s naturally resulted in smugglers becoming more and more desperate: they had to run their goods ashore like commandos, all armed to the teeth, and ready to fight every inch of the way. They came up against not only the coast guards but also the former riding officers, although these were nothing like their former selves: they were now attached to Coast Guard stations and came under the orders of the chief officers. They were known as the Mounted Guard; the Coast Guard directors would not have been so foolhardy as to expect their entirely naval personnel to have anything to do with horses! Now only young cavalry officers were recruited; they were given military ranks, and everything went fairly well for a few years, until the ever-vigilant Treasury stepped in once again and pointed out how costly the Mounted Guard was to maintain. So the Coast Guard bowed to the inevitable and agreed to reduce the mounted force and place the survivors in some of the old, notorious smuggling black-spots.

By the late 1830s the Coast Guard was being hailed as a success in the war against the smugglers, a struggle which had been going on for such a long time and which had cost the country so much, both in its prosecution and in the revenue which the smugglers had denied the Exchequer of successive governments. However, the game was by no means over: the smugglers were still in business and the tighter the service's grip on the coastal counties became, the more determined the free traders seemed to grow. Much of this resistance was by now a matter of tradition and regional pride, as though the smugglers were saying 'How dare they stop us following the trade of our forebears?'

Cornish juries were still, like those of other counties, failing to convict smugglers. In 1835 two coast guards from the Fowey station were on watch on 'Lantic Hill, where they lay concealed under gorse-bushes. Half an hour before midnight they heard a huge party of men, whom they saw were armed with, among other weapons, the old, traditional smugglers' bats. From their eerie the coast guards listened as the party descended to the beach. At this point one of the guards ran for assistance, as their instructions advised. The remaining coast guard gingerly crawled to the edge of the cliff, but, the night being so dark, he could see no one below him. While he was wondering what to do next, he was relieved to hear his comrades approaching, so he fired his pistol to guide them to where he was. Once united with his reinforcements he led the coast guards off after the smugglers, whom they challenged and invited to hand over their smuggled goods. The free traders calmly replied that if the guards laid a single finger on man or tub, they would all be murdered instantly. The coast guards attacked and a ferocious scuffle ensued, one coast guard being knocked unconscious to the ground with a bat, but the smugglers ran off leaving three of their number prisoners; two more were picked up later.

The local cutter had been on station nearby and, on hearing of the affray, its captain had sent a boat in to collect the contraband – 484 gallons of brandy – and the prisoners. These smugglers were put up at the Cornwall summer assizes for 'assisting others in landing and carrying away prohibited goods, some being armed with offensive weapons'. The defence's main claim was that the bats carried by the accused were nothing more than countrymen's walking-sticks, the people in the dock having only been going for a midnight stroll in the pitch dark along a dangerous cliff! A local vicar was actually called to give one of the smugglers a character reference. The rest of the miscreants had a whole parade of local farmers to speak for them.

The judge did his best, saying that what the smugglers had done was 'injurious to the community, and to the fair and honest dealer', and pointed out that the accused could well have been before him on a murder charge. However, the jury were loyal to their own and declared them not guilty, and claimed that their sticks could in no way be construed as being offensive weapons. The smugglers were discharged at once.[6]

A much stranger story of the acquittal of a smuggler happened in 1851 when smuggling was really on its last legs, particularly in Cornwall, the county in which this episode occurred. It seems that a notorious smuggling captain from St Ives, James Williams, brought over a load of whisky from Ireland, of all places, and put it straight on board several fishing smacks beached by the breakwater: this was to be his store while waiting for shipping on, as well as several pigsties on the shore nearby, in an area known as 'Pig's Town'. On the next convenient night the whisky was loaded aboard three waggons which the captain had organized, and these were driven eastwards out of town.

The bold captain had opted for the cheeky exit and all might have gone well with his impudent run, but, as luck would have it, sitting quietly in the snug parlour of the George and Dragon Inn, in the town's market-place, was a coast guard. He heard the rumble of the waggons, went to the window to see what was afoot, ran out and, rather foolishly, tried to halt the convoy. Realizing he had been rumbled, Captain Williams pulled up, grabbed the guard with the help of an accomplice, bound and gagged him, left him helpless by the roadside and carried on with his run. The guard freed himself from his bonds and roused his officer, apprising him of what had happened. This worthy rode after the smugglers, and, at the first toll-house, asked the toll-keeper if any waggons had passed. The answer was, of course, no, for a bribe had been passed; the frustrated officer wheeled his horse around and galloped off towards Penzance, to where he assumed his quarry had gone. However, he was mistaken and the scent was cold.

The next day the officer decided to board Captain Williams's ship, the *St George*, which was anchored in the bay. He found it deserted except for the cabin-boy, who appeared to be a foreigner of some description. Every question was met with 'I do not know', for the smuggler had trained the boy well, threatening to string him up on the yard-arm if he gave any information whatsoever to the coast guards. The officer's next call was on his colleague at the port's Customs house, where they decided to detain the *St George* on the pretext that her name, painted on the stern, was obscured, and that the boat had neither the name of the captain nor the name of its vessel, as the law required.

When he found out what had happened to his ship, Captain Williams took the very unusual step of writing to the local paper, in which a report of the incident had appeared. After outlining the background to the incident, during which he made himself out to be the captain of a simple fishing-smack, Williams went on:

> The general belief in this town and neighbourhood is, that as one of the Coast Guard, named Cock, was rambling from a public-house late on Saturday night, he fancied he met a waggon loaded with contraband goods, and on his attempt to stop the waggon, was either knocked down, or from some other cause, fell under the waggon. This circumstance has caused the detention of my vessel, as at that time she was the only one in the bay. The vessel is still under an arrest, and I very much doubt whether I shall not lose the confidence of my employers unless this business is thoroughly explained; how far they have a right to detain the ship I am at a loss to conceive. Had this occurred in any other port I should with my crew be in a state of very great distress. I am a native of this port and am in consequence thrown upon my friends for my daily bread. . . .

The result of this impudent piece of press publicity was the release of the ship by the Customs a few days later. However, Captain Williams did not leave St Ives immediately; he should have done, for his own sake, for a few days later his vessel was again seized as the Coast Guard and Customs officers had recovered a quantity of kegs from the sea-bottom by the usual method of creeping. The officers matched the tub-rope and a length of chain with pieces on board the *St George*, and on the basis of this evidence they had Captain Williams committed for trial as a smuggler. However, the key witness, the cabin-boy, who turned out to be German, stuck to his story that he had had no idea what went on during the night in question and the case had to be thrown out of court. Such were the disappointments which zealous coast guards and Customs officers had to face as this scientific age of smuggling reached its end.[7]

The pitched battles weren't over yet; it is generally reckoned that the last one was the worst. This took place at Pevensey, Sussex, and is still referred to as the Battle of Pevensey Sluice. Coast guards spotted a landing being made on the beach near the sluice. They converged on the spot, but found that the run was enforced, with a strong guard of musket-men keeping up a constant fusillade so that the guards had to keep their distance. When the smugglers began to withdraw from the beach a running fight with the coast guards began which went on for roughly two hours as they were chased about 8 miles inland. It finished up with three smugglers shot dead and five taken as prisoners. The guards suffered no casualties, but the rest of the smugglers managed to escape across the marshes with the assistance of a fortuitous cloud of fog which had descended. The operation was judged a success for the Coast Guard and did much to put an end to runs of any size in this area, one of the most notorious stretches of coast, for it had been here that two of the worst gangs had held sway for many years, those from Mayfield and Groombridge.[8]

In 1856 the Coast Guard was taken under Admiralty control completely, and the Customs service was left as a much smaller and an entirely unarmed force. The Coast Guard had always been, since its inception, expected to assist ships which were found to be in distress on the coasts which its men patrolled, and to save lives where possible, as far as their main duty of chasing smugglers allowed. It often happened that people on ships drowned or were smashed to pieces on rocks only a stone's throw from the shore and safety. The great problem was getting lines to them over rocks, through mountainous surf, and in the teeth of the highest winds.

As smuggling declined life-saving work grew in the Coast Guard, but why *did* smuggling decline? In part it was due to the aggressive tactics of the service, but it was predominantly because of one man, Sir Robert Peel. Peel was born in 1788, and his first office was chief secretary for Ireland from 1812 to 1818; his chief claim to fame, however, was as a financial wizard. He recommended a return to the gold standard which alarmed his party, and his advocacy of free trade worried it even more. He was a disciple of the great William Huskisson, president of the Board of Trade, who strongly pushed for free trade, and, indeed, set the ball rolling by introducing preferential treatment of goods from the colonies. It was Huskisson's tragically early death in one of the first railway accidents, when he was run over by a locomotive, which postponed his planned all-out attack on restrictive practices. Peel resolved to carry on where his mentor had left off and, over the years, carried out his policy of tariff reforms, which were crowned by the famous repeal of the Corn Laws. Peel must have taken notice of the comments of Captain Hornsby, the commander-general of the Coast Guard, who wrote, when dealing with the duty on tobacco:

> Unless you take the duty off altogether, you would not prevent smuggling. I know the habits and practices of the fishermen along the coasts of Kent and Sussex contiguous to France: they would carry on smuggling however small the duty, because they have greater facilities for it than the fair trader. They get their living by working in boats, they have no port dues to pay, they have no lights to pay, and have none of the expenses attending upon merchant vessels, therefore they would undersell the fair trader even if the duty was low.

This very profound summation of the continuing smuggling problem cannot have gone unnoticed, and on the other side Peel himself said of the Customs service in 1843: 'I confess I distrust everything about the Customs, so far as to feel assured that a vast many have been dishonest and none have been vigilant.' Peel came to power as prime minister in 1841, and found that the Treasury was practically empty. He also discovered that Britain had a real poverty problem for one in eleven people was a true pauper. The Conservatives' predecessors, the Whigs, had not bothered about the poor, or much else, for that matter, certainly not finance, but Peel was born of industrial stock and knew the importance of a sound fiscal and economic policy. His predecessor as prime minister had been Lord Melbourne, who had failed to balance the budget for five years running! The government's main source of revenue at this time was the duties collected by the Customs and Excise services;

as we know this led to wholesale smuggling for decades. If Peel increased these duties he would get more money into the Exchequer, but he knew that this would make many people go without goods they needed and would make the smugglers even happier. So he took the bold step that was so typical of the man: he *lowered* duties in order to encourage people to buy more and more of the taxed goods. He knew that this would lead to higher revenue, more trade and a consequent greater prosperity for the country's vital manufacturing industries. In his budgets of 1842 and 1845, which *he* introduced instead of the chancellor of the Exchequer, Peel abolished completely the duties on over six hundred commodities, and on the articles which were still subject to tax he significantly reduced the duty. Free trade was at once stimulated and prosperity gradually increased, but Peel needed to find other sources of revenue to make good the temporary loss on Customs and Excise. Therefore, Peel revived income tax, which Pitt had first levied during the wars against Napoleon and which had been abandoned in 1816. These measures enabled Peel to balance his budgets easily, and he also actually remitted taxation at the rate of £2½ million a year. The economists who had long argued that the only way to finish smuggling was to reduce the Customs and Excise duties had been vindicated for the traffic in contraband declined noticeably. Peel died as the result of a riding accident in 1850, but his most important work in the cause of beating the smugglers had been completed. There is certainly little doubt that he was able to do far more than his great predecessor William Pitt to end the traffic in contraband which had been such a threat to Britain for so many years, and which had led to her being, in many parts of the world, a laughing-stock, as well as an object of pity 'of less happier lands'.[9]

In 1857 the Board of Customs issued a report of great importance; its most significant passage reads:

With the reduction of duties and the removal of all needless and vexatious restrictions, smuggling has greatly diminished and the public sentiments with regard to it have undergone a very considerable change. The smuggler is no longer an object of public sympathy, or a hero of romance, and people are beginning to awake to the perception of the fact that this offence is less a fraud on the Revenue than a robbery of the fair trader. Smuggling proper is almost entirely

confined to tobacco, spirits and watches; though lace, silk and other
trifling articles are still occasionally seized on the person, or in the
baggage of some unprincipled or inconsiderate passengers; but all
these cases are on the decrease, and in the last ten years have
diminished to about one third. The thoughtless habit, however, of so

Will Watch: a popular Staffordshire pottery figure, as well as the subject of a
well-loved romantic ballad

packing dutiable articles within the folds of ladies' dresses as to answer this purpose, or at least to give the appearance of fraudulent concealment, still prevails among passengers arriving from abroad, and gives rise to many disagreeable disputes. This practice is the more indefensible because the very parties who thus dishonourably

A popular romantic print of smugglers attacked by men of the Coastal Blockade Service (HM Customs & Excise)

endeavour to frustrate the purpose of a partial, rapid and polite search are the loudest and most vehement in their complaint, if that search be minute or tedious.

Old habits die hard, and smuggling was no exception. As late as the year 1868 the inveterate smugglers of the Isle of Wight were still landing spirits, the last seizure being made by the Customs as late as 1874. But the real traffic, in terms of volume, was dwindling to a trickle by the early years of Queen Victoria's reign; and because the people whom he had served, and many whom he had not, were so attached to the smuggler, musicians, painters, poets and potters started turning out images of the 'honest thieves' which found immediate popularity.

'Will Watch, the Bold Smuggler' was a sentimental ballad, with a haunting tune, written by John Davy, the composer of the even more celebrated work 'The Bay of Biscay'. At the same time the famous Staffordshire pottery brought out a figure of Will, and this was soon gracing parlours throughout the land where the ballad telling his stirring story was being sung. Will was said to have been a real life person; but his appearance in the pottery version showed him larger than life: his romantic Byronic shirt revealing his manly chest, his cummerbund more suited to an Italian bandit, his full-cut floral drawers, his beard and moustachios, his sea-boots, pistol and barrel of brandy. However, he took his place on British mantlepieces alongside such folk heroes as Robin Hood, Rob Roy, Nelson and Dick Turpin. And on the walls of these parlours 'penny plain and twopence coloured' prints were hung showing, for example, scenes of smugglers being attacked in their cave by men of the Coastal Blockade and looking more like the pirates of romance, a role in which they now firmly belong.

NOTES

Chapter One

1. *Literary Recollections*, Richard Warner (Longmans, Rees, Orme, Browne & Green, 1830).
2. *The Salisbury and Winchester Chronicle*, 19 March 1779.
3. *Something to Declare: 1,000 Years of Customs and Excise*, Graham Smith (Harrap, 1980).
4. Ibid.
5. *The Wealth of Nations*, Adam Smith (Everyman, 1776).
6. Charles Lamb, 'Essays of Elia', *London Magazine*, vol. III (1833).
7. John Wesley, *Journals* (Methodist Society, London, 1791).
8. Shelburne Documents, House of Commons Library.
9. Smith, *Something to Declare*.

Chapter Two

1. Smith, *Something to Declare*.
2. Graham Smith, 'The Great Anti-Smuggler', *Dorset: the County Magazine*, 101 (1982).
3. Letter-books, Poole Customs House, HM Customs & Excise Library, London.
4. *At War with the Smugglers*, D. Arnold Forster (Conway Maritime Press, 1936).
5. Red House Museum Library, Christchurch, Hampshire County Council.
6. 'Instructions to Riding Supervisors and Officers of Customs' (1734), HM Customs and Excise Library, London.

7.   Abraham Pike, Journal for 1803 and 1804 (County Records Office, Dorchester).

8.   *Smuggling in Hampshire and Dorset: 1700 to 1850*, Geoffrey Morley (Countryside Books, Newbury, 1983).

9.   *Smuggling in Kent and Sussex: 1700–1840*, Mary Waugh (Countryside Books, Newbury, 1985).

Chapter Three

1.   Waugh, *Smuggling in Kent and Sussex*.
2.   *Life of Samuel Johnson*, James Boswell (Oxford, 1791).
3.   *Contraband Cargoes*, Neville Williams (Longmans, Green & Co., London, 1959).
4.   *The Diary of a Country Parson: 1758 to 1802*, Revd James Woodforde (OUP, 1978).
5.   Hervey Papers, HM Customs & Excise Library, London (1735).
6.   Smith, *Something to Declare*.

Chapter Four

1.   *Honest Thieves*, Frederick Nicholls (Heinemann, 1973).
2.   *A Midsummer Night's Dream*, William Shakespeare.
3.   Williams, *Contraband Cargoes*.
4.   Waugh, *Smuggling in Kent and Sussex*.

Chapter Five

1.   Waugh, *Smuggling in Kent and Sussex*.
2.   Morley, *Smuggling in Hampshire and Dorset*.
3.   Admiralty Letter Book, Admiral Edward Vernon (1740).
4.   Waugh, *Smuggling in Kent and Sussex*.
5.   *Smugglers' Britain*, G. Bernard Wood (Cassell, London, 1966).
6.   *A Book about Smuggling in the West Country: 1700–1850*,

Antony D. Hippisley Coxe (Tabb House, Padstow, Cornwall, 1984).

7. *The Scilly Isles*, C.C. Vyvyan (Robert Hale, 1960).
8. Williams, *Contraband Cargoes*.
9. *Smuggling on Wight Island*, R.F.W. Dowling (published by the author, 1978).
10. *Yarmouth*, Captain John Cole (published by the author, 1960).

Chapter Six

1. *Coast Guard*, C. Webb (HMSO, 1980).
2. Smith, *Something to Declare*.
3. Ibid.

Chapter Seven

1. Smith, *Something to Declare*.
2. Webb, *Coast Guard*.
3. 'General Instructions for the Coast Guard of the United Kingdom', HM Customs & Excise Library, London (1829).
4. *The Smugglers of Christchurch, Bourne Heath and the New Forest*, E. Russell Oakley (Hutchinson & Co., 1944).
5. *The Smuggler's Guide to Purbeck*, Clive R. Hardy (published by the author, 1980).
6. *Tales of the Cornish Smugglers*, John Vivian (Tor Mark Press, Truro, Cornwall, 1978).
7. Ibid.
8. Waugh, *Smuggling in Kent and Sussex*.
9. *The Makers of English History*, Frank Prochaska (Weidenfeld and Nicolson, London, 1987).

INDEX